MARY THE MOTHER OF GOD

IS VOLUME

44

OF THE

Twentieth Century Encyclopedia of Catholicism

UNDER SECTION

IV

THE MEANS OF REDEMPTION

IT IS ALSO THE

27TH

VOLUME IN ORDER OF PUBLICATION

Edited by HENRI DANIEL-ROPS of the Académie Française

MARY THE MOTHER
OF GOD

By L. J. SUENENS

Translated from the French by
A NUN OF STANBROOK ABBEY

HAWTHORN BOOKS · PUBLISHERS · *New York*

First Edition, October, 1959
Second Printing, March, 1961
Third Printing, April, 1962

NIHIL OBSTAT

Adrianus van Vliet, S.T.D.

    Censor deputatus

IMPRIMATUR

E. Morrogh Bernard,

    Vicarius Generalis

Westmonasterii, die XXVI MAII, MCMLIX

CUM PERMISSU SUPERIORUM O.S.B.

CONTENTS

INTRODUCTION

The liturgy of the feast of the Assumption puts upon the lips of the angels appointed to receive Mary into heaven this wondering question: "Who is this, whose coming shows like the dawn of day? No moon so fair, no sun so majestic, no embattled array so awes men's hearts." [1]

Men also inquire concerning her, and Catholics of the twentieth century more than others. The consecration of the world to Mary Immaculate in the second world war, the definition of the dogma of the Assumption, the proclamation of the Queenship of Mary, the Marian year, the centenary celebrations of the apparitions at Lourdes, all events which took place during the pontificate of Pius XII, compel our contemporaries to observe her and ask likewise, "Who is this?"

The faithful long to know her better, to acquire a more enlightened knowledge of one whom they feel is both so universal and so near, who belongs to the whole world and is yet so accessible to the individual. This book aims at satisfying this eager desire of Mary's children. Without entering into the details of theological controversies, it is addressed to all Catholics in order that they may come to understand their Mother better by giving her a larger place in their lives. The writer's principal care has been to make clear the divine idea and plan with respect to our Lady, to point out the place and the rôle destined for her by God, for that is all-important. For what does she stand in the eyes of God? Why and how did he will Mary to be?

[1] Song of Songs 6. 9.

True devotion to Mary takes its rise not from below but from above: not from feelings of affection but from faith. In the first place it means clinging to God and accepting his design, and it is an integral element of our right intention with respect to him since Christian rectitude begins by voluntarily accepting the plan he has willed, by cooperating with him who has traced out, as he sees fit, the direction of his grace. God has willed to associate Mary with his work of salvation and by her he has given his Son to the world. Now the gifts of God are without recall and this "order" remains unchangeable. Mary's mediatory position remains for ever, for such is the divine plan.

With what love did our Lord, who always did his Father's will, enter the world in the manner designed for him by his Father! We, who are his disciples, must not hesitate to be of his mind with respect to Mary. Since it is God who chose her for his Son and for us, we have no choice but to receive her as our Mother. We are attracted by her beauty and goodness, and we feel the need to turn to her, but we are happy in yielding ourselves, in the first place, in virtue of obedience to the divine will. Such supremely is the reason for our devotion to Mary. It is not for us to set limits to the divine action or to dispense with the intermediaries which God has freely chosen. It belongs to him to love us with a love surpassing all understanding and measure, and to glorify his creatures by making them his instruments. In God there is room for every kind of superabundance, and it is only at our level that restriction or niggardliness is to be found. The filial cultus we render to Mary is only an expression of thanksgiving for the prodigality of divine love of which she is the living and abiding witness. It would be quite erroneous to regard the piety we bear towards her as a useless excrescence which interferes with our worship of God. Nor is that piety a sort of sentimental superfluity, a concession to the imagination and to popular feeling and an easy means of securing salvation. For all, without distinction, it is the expression of God's will in our regard.

Devotion to Mary is a law of God, but she is also a gift to us, and this expression of the divine will hides a mystery of love. After Christ himself, she is the most outstanding of God's graces: "If thou knewest what it is God gives!" [2] said our Lord to the Samaritan woman. In that gift Mary is included, for the mystery of the Son includes that of the Mother, and we must not hesitate to accept from the hand of God her who is thus offered to us. To each one of us God has repeated, in a sense, the words of the angel to Joseph: "Do not be afraid to take thy wife, Mary, to thyself, for it is by the power of the Holy Spirit that she has conceived this child." [3]

THE MEANING OF THE THEOLOGICAL CONTROVERSIES

The laity should not be surprised that theologians have not yet completed their study of this mystery. Theologians have an indispensable part to play; it is for them to search into the deposit of faith, to draw up an inventory of its riches and harmonies, to clarify its truths by relating one to the other and to try to synthesize them, as also to restrain whatever exaggerations due to a fanciful, unbalanced piety may have crept into sound doctrine.

Far from being scandalized at the conflict between certain theological opinions which, however, as we shall see, are very circumscribed, we should discern in them the general effort to enter ever more deeply into the mind of God as it is expressed in tradition, whether oral or written. As the builders of cathedrals erected flying buttresses

[2] John 4. 10.
[3] Matt. 1. 20.

and pointed vaulting, one against the other, so do theologians work together in the Church at a common task, even when each of them stresses truths which are complementary one to another. As collaborators in a work for the Church, which goes beyond them and yet unites them, they serve the Catholic community and the hierarchical *magisterium* to which it belongs to give the decisive teaching, authentically guaranteed. The history, for example, of the evolution of the doctrine of the Immaculate Conception, when theologians who, just because they are such do not thereby cease to be human, fought fiercely in order to defend either the universal redemption of mankind by Christ or the anticipated and privileged redemption of Mary, illustrates what we have been saying of these doctrinal thrusts and counter-thrusts which the Church at the time willed by God directs towards a higher synthesis, which eradicates views that are too one-sided by associating them together.

It may happen that the supernatural instinct of the faithful anticipates the explicit and always laborious definition of the dogma. That simply proves that, according to the Master's promise, the Holy Spirit is working in all his children, in the simplest as well as in the most learned, but we must be grateful to the theologians whose barrages have raised the level of the waters and strengthened their fruitful impetuosity. The fullness of truth is the gainer thereby.

The present study aims at helping all the children of the Church, layfolk as well as clergy, the better to understand the mystery and the providential rôle of Mary, in order that their Catholic life may be increasingly enlightened by her and developed to its highest degree. We confine ourselves to treating of its essential riches, its highest graces, without hoping to exhaust the subject.

CHAPTER I

THE THRESHOLD

OF THE MYSTERY

Holy Scripture relates how when Moses came to Mount Horeb he saw the angel of God revealed to him under the form of a flame of fire breaking forth from a bush. As he looked, he saw that although the bush was burning it was not being consumed, and he wished to approach nearer in order to examine the phenomenon; but God called to him from the centre of the bush and thus commanded him: "Do not come nearer; rather take the shoes from thy feet, thou are standing on holy ground." [1]

Tradition has likened Mary to that bush which, although on fire, was not destroyed. Having become a mother without ceasing to be a virgin, she bore within her that flame of fire that is the living God, and our Lord's presence in Mary made her, as it were, a living sanctuary, a holy place, not to be approached save with infinite respect and after having stripped ourselves of ideas that are too human.

GOD'S PARADISE

We are entering upon a world that is not at our level, and penetrating into the realm of God's unfathomable

[1] Exod. 3. 5.

love. It is true that our Lady is a created being. Of herself
she is nothing, just as we all are, and there is no need to
labour so obvious a fact. But she has been completely
overwhelmed with the divine love, like a torrent falling
into an abyss, and we shall have to measure the height and
depth and breadth of that divine charity that is at work
in her. That amounts to saying that we can approach the
mystery of Mary only by means of a grace of enlightenment by the Holy Spirit who alone searches into the deep
things of God, and go forward, as did the High Priest of
the old Law, beyond the veil into the innermost sanctuary.

In order that we may understand Mary, it is necessary
for God to create in us a certain affinity with her and to
purify our outlook. As St John says, "How can the man
who has no love have any knowledge of God," [2] and this
is true also in the case of Mary. Hence it is not surprising
that through the ages those who can best help us to understand her have been the saints. They are witnesses that
our Lord's words are as true as ever, and that God always
sees fit to reveal these things to the humble and to "little
ones." Everything taught by modern philosophy as to the
intervention of the qualities of heart and mind applies
especially in this connection. We need great delicacy of
perception, purity and freshness of mind if we are to enter
into this realm of light and love. A saint who entered very
far has called Mary "the paradise and unspeakable world
of God," and states that God made a world for the trav-
eller, our own: that he made one for the blessed, heaven:
and that he made one for himself which he called Mary.
Nor is this merely poetic sentimentality, but a statement
made after mature reflection, which may help us, if necessary, to understand why our Lord devoted thirty years
of his life to increasing continually in his Mother the

[2] I John 4. 8.

fullness of her first grace, for the glory of the Blessed Trinity.

PROGRESSIVE REVELATION

That same sanctity explains why the mystery of Mary was to be revealed only gradually. In each one of us this discovery will follow the rule of the slow progress which holds good through the course of history for the whole Church, and it will take place under the same impetus of love.

We know that divine revelation was closed finally after the death of St John, the last of the Apostles. No new dogma will make its appearance in the Church; all the truths of our faith are for ever contained in the deposit of revelation, but under the enlightenment of the Holy Spirit our knowledge of the faith can go on increasing and intensifying from age to age. This fresh knowledge can be compared to the successive discoveries of certain stars which have taken place. The stars existed from the beginning, but their light shone into human eyes only after centuries of movement and according to light waves of differing lengths. Our Lord himself prepared us for this gradual growth of supernatural truth when he told his Apostles: "I have still much to say to you, but it is beyond your reach as yet. It will be for him, the truth-giving Spirit, when he comes, to guide you into all truth." [3] Therefore our Lord was reserving to the Holy Spirit the task of leading the Apostles to the fullness of truth.

This ever deepening understanding of the truths of religion God has entrusted not only to our intellects, enlightened by faith, but also to our love or, to speak more precisely, to our loving understanding, moved by the will

[3] John 16. 12–13.

and continually vivified by practice and action. Not that love is in juxtaposition to the work of the intellect, but it stimulates the latter from within, ever urging it on to investigate and possess what it loves. Love wants to read within—*intus legere*—and aspires to know; it wants to co-exist with what it loves: to take in all the outlines, search into all the folds, attain to the final secret of an existence. Nor is love satisfied so long as a single reaction escapes it, so long as everything is not an open book. For love nothing is too small, too trifling, nothing is merely an accessory. It acts like the player who stakes his fortune on every move he makes. That is why love longs to know everything, to explore everything, to have everything clear since, as says Pascal, we do not really know anyone unless we know everything about him. Truth and love are too intimately connected for a soul to be able to draw near to the one without the support of the other, and their twofold and yet single progress should mark the stages of even our spiritual searching.

Nor is love only a matter of feeling but of willing and faithful activity. Love means putting into action what is in the will, making real and effective the will to do right. Nor is such action as it were alien to the understanding of the divine mysteries. Maurice Blondel expressed this link between spirit and life unusually well when he wrote: "Action informed by faith is the ark of the covenant wherein dwell the divine secrets. What Christ has sought and obtained is not, in the first place, to be investigated like a theological theorem but to be loved above all else."

All this is true to the letter with respect to the progressive discovery of Mary. Sincere love of her leads us to study her glories and her mission, and such filial piety also needs to be enlightened. It needs to learn all the glory of God that is immanent in his Mother, to scrutinize her countenance, so to speak, and recognize the tone of her voice. A devotion to Mary which does not lead us to study her very soon fades away, and is reduced to superficial emotion or routine. Every right-minded child wants to know its mother, because it loves her and wants to love her more. Hence, there is opened up before us a wide field for spreading doctrinal teaching concerning our Lady. Priests, religious, lay Catholic leaders, teachers at every level, all have the duty of leading those entrusted to them to the dogmatic sources of devotion to Mary. It is for them to raise the standard of such devotion, so as to make it coincide as far as possible with the mind of God. Then, but only then, will it be "like a tree planted by running water, ready to yield its fruit when the season comes, not a leaf faded." [4]

Nor must there be any fear lest this doctrinal study will do harm to love, for that could happen only if the actual study had become perverted because it was separated from love. Dogmatic truth can be productive only of life, unless a soul fails to recognize the truth and betrays it. In order, however, that the truth may be spirit and life, it is not enough to study it only for its own sake and in itself. Progressively it must become rooted in an attitude of life which assimilates it and incorporates it. If a soul is to go from glory to glory it must make steady progress towards an ever increasing fidelity. In the measure in which we allow Mary's motherhood to act in us, we shall find out its true meaning. Knowing means life.

Moreover, we do not discover Mary for our own sakes alone. As our Lady of the Visitation hastened to her kinswoman, Elizabeth, in order to share with the latter the secret of her joy, so must we hasten to transform the light we have received into a warmth of fervour which can be communicated to others. If we wish to possess more ourselves, we must give to others; such is the unchanging law

[4] Psalm 1. 3.

of the Gospel. We can keep God's treasures only if we offer them to others, because everything that is of God entails the giving of self. Such must be the attitude of the soul that is beginning to study the mystery of Mary, and only thus can that soul find the right way that leads into that paradise of God.

CHAPTER II

MARY IN THE DIVINE PLAN

MAN IN THE THOUGHT OF GOD

God does not know us because we exist; we exist because he knows us. We are unused to such a perspective because we see things above from below, yet it is from above that all things take their origin, since reality is born from the creative mind of God. As Ravaisson says: "The world is a thought that does not think, suspended from a mind that thinks," and this applies in a still higher degree for the human being who must grasp it at its source. This seems to us a topsy-turvy and roundabout way of proceeding. We avoid seeing things, as the saying is, "in the mirror of God," because we set the two entities, the mirror and the reality, in juxtaposition, which means that we forget that we are only a reflection and a participation of God: that God is more "us" than we are ourselves, and that his creative mind is the source of our being, our vocation, that it defines us and constitutes the centre of our substance.

MARY IN THE THOUGHT OF GOD

This is also true as regards Mary. In order to understand her, we must go back in thought to the beginning of the world, to God's creative mind. In the last analysis, why did God create the world?

St Paul replies: for Christ. He it is, indeed, who is the beginning and the end, the last word on everything. In him creation holds together, he is the keystone of the arch, the supreme why and wherefore. Everything, heaven and earth, things visible and invisible, history, space, all has been made in view of our Lord Jesus Christ. As says St Paul: "He has chosen us out, in Christ, before the foundation of the world, to be saints, to be blameless in his sight for love of him; marking us out beforehand (so his will decreed) to be his adopted children through Jesus Christ. Thus he would manifest the splendour of that grace by which he has taken us into his favour in the person of his beloved Son." [1] It is in Christ, the Incarnate Word, that the world acquires its meaning, its stability and its finality, and in him the key to the dialectic of history is to be found. In the mystery of Christmas, with all that flows from it, lies all our philosophy or, better still, our theology of the story of creation.

But if the Incarnation lies at the heart of God's creative action, it is Mary who makes that Incarnation possible, and therein lies her incomparable greatness. Her motherhood is the answer to the Incarnation of the Word, and from that essential and vital link begins the chain of the other mysteries. The mysterious origin of the Blessed Virgin, declared Pius IX in the Bull *Ineffabilis,* was foreseen and ordained by one and the same decree with the Incarnation of the divine Wisdom.

This link is unbreakable. It might even possibly exist independently of the redemption of the world. We know that according to many theologians before and after St Thomas Aquinas, the Incarnation, and so the divine motherhood, have as their principal object the redemption

[1] Ephes. 1. 4–6.

of mankind, which implies that had original sin not existed the Word would not have become man. But another strong theological current of opinion holds, with Duns Scotus, that if, in the present order of things, the Incarnation was in fact a redemption, Christ came into this world above all as its Lord and as the crowning glory of creation, and that even had Adam not sinned the Son of God would have become incarnate in Mary's womb. According to this conception, which is that of St Albert the Great, Scheeben and Mgr Gay, Christ appeared, and Mary in him, as willed by God, before every creature, as the summit of the creation which is ordered in view of him. According to this view, God decreed from the beginning to create, in Christ and for him, the jewel that is Mary with the world as the casket.

Whether or no this may be, even if in God the decision of the Incarnation was subsequent to original sin, the former once decreed makes everything converge towards her, just as by its attraction the sea controls the course of the rivers. When an artist sets out to design a fresco, he first decides upon the chief personages, and then, on account of them and to make them stand out, draws in the rest of his scene; light and shadow, foreground and background, the different perspectives, landscape and sky. The incomparable artist, God, willed the whole creation in view of Christ and consequently in view of Mary, since in the divine plan Christ was not conceived without Mary. For her sake was created the brilliance of the sun, the fairyland of the stars and the planets, as ornaments of her glory. For her, the earth as her footstool; for her, the mountains and the plains, the oceans and the rivers, and the blue sky which was to be the image of her queenly mantle. All was for her, because she is the first-born of creatures in Christ. Because she is at the heart of the Incarnation, the liturgy does not hesitate to apply to her the passage of Scripture which, in the first place, refers to the divine Wisdom. On the feast of Mary's Nativity, as on that of her Immaculate Conception, the Church puts on her lips this passage:

> The Lord made me when first he went about his work, at the birth of time, before his creation began. Long, long ago, before earth was fashioned, I held my course. Already I lay in the womb, when the depths were not yet in being, when no springs of water had yet broken; when I was born, the mountains had not yet sunk on their firm foundations, and there were no hills; not yet had he made the earth or the rivers, or the solid framework of the world. I was there when he built the heavens, when he fenced in the waters with a vault inviolable, when he fixed the sky overhead, and levelled the fountain-springs of the deep. I was there when he closed the sea within its confines, forbidding the waters to transgress their assigned limits, when he poised the foundations of the world. I was at his side, a master-workman, my delight increasing with each day, as I made play before him all the while; made play in this world of dust, with the sons of Adam for my playfellows. (Prov. 8. 22–31.)

These are astonishing words which go back into the night of time through which, as we think over the past ages, we see shining an impressive clarity. How can we read that Mary's delight is to be with the sons of Adam without thinking over her work of grace from generation to generation in the soul of every Christian? But let us not anticipate. At present we are concerned only to understand the place that is hers in the initial plan of God before the world was created.

MARY IN THE HEART OF GOD

God loves us all and with all the intensity of his being, with the maximum power of his love. He loves each one of us. He gives himself as God, ever equal to himself. He is not more or less loving, just as he is not more or less present in the Blessed Sacrament. His is a total giving. A God who would bestow a half or a third of his love would not be God. Faith, which reveals to us the Triune God, teaches us that the Father gives himself wholly in the Word and that together both give themselves wholly in the Holy Spirit. It is in the Incarnate Word that he loves us all with the divine plenitude.

Nevertheless, creatures and their vocations are not equal; the gifts received from God are not identical in every case. That is true, but the inequality does not arise from the fact that the initial love bestowed was not equal. The inequality of the divine favours bestowed is to be measured, from the side of God, the giver, according to the place which he is reserving for us in his kingdom, in his mystical Body; while from the side of man, who is the receiver, it depends upon the degree of receptivity. As far as we can see, everything goes to show that, on this twofold plane, after the humanity of Jesus Christ, Mary is the first.

We are all called by God to be his children and the co-heirs of his kingdom, and it is impossible for a man to be more or less a son. The only difference is in the part God destines each one to play, and which contains for that one the maximum of his love. Our deficiencies are due to our want of correspondence with the designs he has for us, and once a soul has grasped wherein lies human inequality, it understands better the play of the divine predilection. God loves us all equally without reserve, but the degrees of intimacy and the expression of that love will vary according to the souls' receptivity, rather as a spring pours forth its waters into different vessels according to their shape and the sizes of their openings.

What confers upon Mary her peerless rank is her capacity for corresponding to the divine love; the abyss she offers to that divine outpouring. No creature, angelic or

human, can receive that love as she can; not one has cor-
responded as she has to the divine advances. She is wholly
surrendered to God's good pleasure, and in her he has
been able to realize the perfect work of his creation. He
has looked upon her with a special love. Nor is such a predilection to be compared to a human preference. When
God chooses a soul for an especially high mission, that
same mission is of benefit to all. The love for one individual is immediately changed into a universal love. Far from
excluding others, his choice involves them; what is a
single good becomes a common good and affects the world
at large.

We find it hard to understand this implication, since
for us human beings a choice supposes a preference, and
to prefer implies, willy-nilly, that he who has the preference relegates to a lower plane what is not chosen, that he
rejects what with him is not an object of predilection.
Every favour shown to the chosen is a choice made, in a
sense, to the detriment of the rejected; at the least, the
latter is put aside. But, once more, there is nothing like
that with God. His preference is not to the detriment of
others, and deprives them of nothing. On the contrary,
they gain by that preference in that they are included in
the dispensation of grace which it assures to all. God has
chosen someone; the elect receives a higher vocation; the
reach of that vocation will be more universally extended.
The higher the spring, the better its waters are distributed.

That Mary is for God a world apart is already a grace
for men and for the angels. Her vocation is already a mystery of mediation and of communion with us, poor mor-
tals. On every side, she is open to the love of God, which
through her draws us nearer to the Father and to our
brethren. In her there is no idea as of a treasure that is
denied, a possession that is exclusive. She gives as much

as she receives, transmits as much as is entrusted to her.

And it is because she is wholly a gift that the Son of God showered spiritual riches upon her during the thirty years of their life together. Mary was overwhelmed with graces, with light; she heard innumerable words to ponder in her heart, but this work of sanctification prepared her in view of her mission as Mother of all living, according to the constant law of God's predilection.

CHAPTER III

THE IMMACULATE CONCEPTION

MARY, THE FULFILMENT OF THE PAST

Mary belongs to both the Old and New Testaments. She closes the Old and completes the past, and she opens the New and inaugurates the fullness of time. Chronologically, her life falls before, during and after the human life of her Son, and she seems destined to be the living transition between each of these phases. She is the link between the people of Israel and the Saviour they are awaiting, and between the new-born Church and the risen Christ, and she anticipates the Parousia by her own Assumption.

Mary, we said, comes at the end of the journey of Israel towards its salvation. The Old Testament is but the record of a long wait for the Redeemer's coming, and that coming is of its nature a journey towards the woman blessed above all the daughters of Israel, whose presence we sense through all the appeals of the patriarchs and the prophets: at first dimly sketched in, as it were, but becoming increasingly clear. The foretelling by Isaias of the Virgin who shall conceive is a bright ray lighting up the obscurity of the inspired words and arousing the hope of a people.

This link between Mother and Son runs, like a golden thread, through the Old Testament. Mary sums up and makes incarnate the long preparation of twenty centuries which preceded the coming of the Messias. God chose Israel to make it the instrument of his designs with respect to other nations, but Israel failed to understand that mission and remained shut up within itself. In Mary, a daughter of Israel, that universal love at last attained its object.

"Not only," writes Fr Daniélou, "is she the daughter of Israel, but she is the one Israelite in whom the race of Israel flows out upon humanity as a whole, for she is both daughter of Abraham and daughter of David and at the same time Mother of divine Grace, universal Mediatrix, Mother of mankind. . . . She it is who consented to be no longer only a Jewess, but to open her heart so as to take in the whole world. . . . Thus at the close of Jewish history, she is truly the perfect success of what God willed to bring about." [1] She is the beloved Israel of God: the Israel truly faithful to the divine idea and to his call.

EXEMPTION FROM ORIGINAL SIN

We have not to follow the stages of this progress towards the Incarnation, but we must pause at the threshold of the latter, at the final preparation, the glorious preface to the divine Motherhood, the Immaculate Conception.

Ill-instructed Catholics sometimes think that the object of this mystery is the actual conception of Mary: in this view Mary was not conceived according to the order of nature; her mother, Anne, conceived while remaining a virgin as later did Mary herself. Now there is no question of Mary's being an exception *in the order of nature*. She was conceived like every child of Adam, her divine Son only excepted, through the ordinary conjugal relation of her father and mother. What is here involved is an exception *in the order of grace*. The privilege of the Immacu-

[1] Jean Daniélou, S.J. *The Mystery of Advent,* London and New York, Sheed and Ward, 1953.

late Conception is that it took place under the sign of grace; from the first moment of her existence in her mother's womb, far from being deprived of the divine friendship and the divine life, Mary was overwhelmed therewith: she was already "full of grace." There we have all the difference between her and the other children of Adam since original sin came into the world. The latter are conceived and born deprived of that very grace which was never wanting to Mary.

As we know, the recognition of this privilege as a dogmatic truth was secured only after keen theological discussion. The age-old controversies about the Immaculate Conception were due to the seeming incompatibility of two truths equally sacred for all Christians. Surely, to declare that Mary was conceived without original sin was equivalent to denying that Christ died to redeem all mankind without exception? Did not Mary's privilege seem to exempt her from the benefit of the redemption? Did it not look like an attack on the faith of the church in the universality of that atonement, as also an exorbitant exception to the necessity of salvation coming by the cross? No one would have had any difficulty in accepting the teaching that, like St John the Baptist, Mary was sanctified in her mother's womb, or immediately after her conception; for such an hypothesis supposes a period, however short, during which Mary was under the thraldom of original sin and, consequently, had to be redeemed like the rest of the human race. It was granted that Mary might have outstripped others on the ordinary road, but was it necessary to go further, and withdraw her from the ordinary condition of other human beings?

In the end, theology found the way out of the *impasse* by showing that, like us, and even more than we, Mary owed everything to the redemption, since for her, and her alone, that redemption took a preventive form.

Pius IX set forth this privilege in precise terms in the Bull *Ineffabilis*, every shade of meaning of which is vital: "For the honour and glory of the holy and undivided Trinity, for the glory and adornment of the Virgin Mother of God, for the exaltation of the Catholic faith, and the increase of the Christian religion, we declare, proclaim, and define, by the authority of our Lord Jesus Christ, of the blessed apostles Peter and Paul, and by our own authority, that the doctrine which maintains that the most blessed Virgin Mary was, in the first instant of her Conception, by the singular grace and privilege of Almighty God, through the foreseen merits of Christ Jesus, Saviour of mankind, preserved immune from all stain of original sin, is revealed by God, and in consequence is to be constantly and firmly believed by all the faithful."

Thus then, while the redemption delivers us from the fatal consequences of original sin, by restoring to us the divine friendship, the same redemption magnificently preserves Mary from a privation which cannot affect her in any way, since, in view of the future sacrifice of the Redeemer, by the power of the blood, and merits of our Lord Jesus Christ, she is created in grace. As the Church tells us, she is "redeemed in a more excellent manner."

Thus is brought about the necessary reconciliation of the two truths. Our Lord is the Saviour of all mankind; his redemption includes all without any exception. Because she was to be the Mother of Christ, the Saviour of the whole human race, Mary was never to know the humiliating privation resulting from Adam's sin. Exempt as she is from the consequences of original sin, she shares in a more excellent manner than all other human beings the blessed effects of the redemption which secures for her so glorious an exception. This doctrinal harmony is the result of the light of the Holy Spirit by which, little by little, the Church's theologians were enabled to abstract the principles demanded by the divine scheme of salvation and construct a synthesis whereby no truth of the Catholic faith was sacrificed.

This privilege of our Lady was proclaimed as a dogma of faith in 1854, by Pius IX, and, as we know, four years later the events at Lourdes echoed the papal definition in a sensational and lasting fashion.

In order to grasp fundamentally the Immaculate Conception, we must return to the original plan of the Creator. "God created us," says St Paul, "to be saints, to be blameless in his sight." [2] Through sin, man spoilt that divine plan, but God was not thereby thwarted in resuming his primary purpose, and he willed to transform his spoilt work into a new creation, of which Mary is the anticipation and the complete realization. From the first instant of her creation, therefore, she was exempt from original sin through the loving-kindness of God who is divinely "impatient" to impart himself, by means of a priority of love which is an abyss of victorious generosity. Mary becomes the type of that Church which, though its human reality is composed of sinners, may yet glorify God for making it holy and blameless in its divine realization.

Mary was, then, from her birth in integrity and perfection what we become when we are baptized. From the first moment of her existence, she was pleasing to the Most High. For the Mother of our Saviour, God's will to save was all-embracing; for the Mother of the Redeemer the redemption was radical from the beginning. Christ was the Redeemer, even to the Immaculate Conception, of his Mother. Although the daughter of a line of sinners, Mary never incurred the sin of her race. It was for her, in the first place, that the blood of her Saviour flowed. She is the eldest daughter of the passion.

[2] Ephes. 1. 4.

By comparing her situation with our own, we understand better how unique she is. She is pure, we have been justified. There is a world of difference between that purity and that purification, as Péguy remarks when he hails in Mary "a certain primeval spotlessness, a certain integrity as of the first innocence of childhood. What is regained, defended foot by foot, won, retaken, won again, is in no wise the same as what has never been lost. A paper that has been whitened is far from being a white paper, and a soul whitened is not a white soul." This privilege places Mary in a world of her own, and clothes her with an innocence unequalled here on earth.

This exemption of Mary from original sin is due exclusively to her quality of Mother of God. That title is incommunicable and that glory cannot be shared with another. For her, God has suspended by a miracle the hereditary contagion of original sin, and he has so done for the sake of him who was to be born of her. The sanctity of the Son is the cause of the anticipated sanctification of the Mother, just as the sun lights up the sky before disappearing below the horizon.

Belief in the sanctity of Mary was asserted in the Church with ever-increasing emphasis, especially after the Council of Ephesus in 431. There were certain Doctors of the first centuries, like St John Chrysostom, who had hesitated on the matter and put forward certain exegetic interpretations unanimously rejected since by both east and west. Even the east, while not explicitly putting the question in relation to a doctrine of original sin, has still more clearly emphasized the complete sanctity, even in her conception, of the Mother of God, and does not hesitate even to multiply hyperbole on top of hyperbole when there is question of honouring the *Panagia*—she who is "all-holy." The eastern churches multiply liturgical feasts of Mary, nearly all of which originated among themselves, and it is no longer possible to count the sermons preached on such occasions, echoing a wonder which can never stale.

As for the west, St Augustine pointed out the way which was followed by the whole Latin tradition when he wrote the celebrated words: "Concerning Mary, for the sake of the honour of God, I absolutely refuse that any question should be raised as regards sin."

FULLNESS OF GRACE

The exemption from original sin, which characterizes the dogma of the Immaculate Conception, might lead us to think that we are here faced with what is only a negative privilege, but such is not the case. It implies immediately a positive result, a fullness of grace and love; it means that the soul is filled to overflowing with the Holy Spirit. It is well to pause here for a moment. No one has better expressed this than Pius IX in the Bull *Ineffabilis Deus,* defining the dogma. It opens with these words: "God . . . chose and ordained, from the beginning and before all ages, a Mother for his only-begotten Son, in whom he should become incarnate and of whom he should be born. . . . And upon her also he bestowed so great a love, beyond that bestowed upon all other creatures, that in her he delighted exceedingly. Wherefore, he so wonderfully adorned her, above all angels and saints, with abundance of all heavenly graces drawn from the treasury of his Godhead that, absolutely free from every stain of sin, all-beautiful and perfect, she might be shown forth in a fullness of innocence and holiness, than which no greater can be imagined, and which, save God, no one can attain to in thought."

When we say that the fullness of Mary's graces surpasses that of all the angels and saints, we may sometimes be tempted to think of a plenitude in a manner that is too exclusively one of quantity. Grace is not like a gold piece which, when added to others, would make up a treasure more or less considerable. That is a mistaken idea. Nor is grace a reality which isolates us and shuts us up in ourselves. On the contrary, it is grace that opens us to God and makes us capable of receiving him. Created grace is inconceivable without uncreated grace; that is, without a God who gives himself and thereby introduces us into his own intimate life: a life that is in action and tends to extend itself abroad. Grace means that the living God imparts himself to us, and in Mary the degree of union with God incomparably surpasses that of all creatures put together, but in its own way it is a matter of quality and not quantity.

Once that is understood, no one is any longer tempted in this connection to talk about exaggeration. We simply respect the incommunicable gift of God to our Lady: the quality of a motherhood that is unique. The fullness of grace in Mary is not that of Jesus. In him that fullness is complete from the beginning and cannot be increased; in her, the fullness is limited and therefore capable of being increased. She received the Holy Spirit at her conception, at the Incarnation and at Pentecost, and each time he wrought for her his wonders. Her life in God of faith, hope and charity knew a progressive development—and how marvellous a development!

COROLLARIES

This fullness of grace involves many consequences. Being the one and only spotless human being, Mary stands out as the masterpiece of creation, and yet she remains perfectly human. How supremely perfect must be her balance, her self-control! Body and soul are in perfect harmony, and the latter is not less perfectly attuned to the

Godhead. The voice of that soul joins the concert of the
Holy Trinity with an unequalled fullness which we must
examine in detail.

The soul in harmony with God

There is in Mary an affinity with God, a delicate sensitiveness to God such as we cannot imagine. God is reflected in her soul as in a glass prism. Everything in her
is referred to him and she is completely at his disposal.
Every fibre of her being, both natural and supernatural,
utters a perpetual "Yes" to his will, and she reflects him
faithfully. Her soul offers itself to him as the keys of an
organ to the hand of the musician, ready to vibrate at the
slightest touch, to seize upon the faintest melody, the least
breath. At every moment her own will coincides with the
divine will, and she yields to his love as a reed bends with
the wind. As the hand, second by second, goes round the
clockface, her will is there, wherever God wishes it to be.
Whereas we are constantly tempted to live in the past or
the future, to the detriment of the full attention we ought
to be giving to the duty of the present moment, Mary
succeeds in that marvel of co-existence, coincidence, of
unceasing communion with God whch is the secret of
holiness. The treatise of Fr Caussade on *Abandonment
to divine Providence* could be constantly illustrated by her
example. In her life, she lived out that *abandon* to the
letter. The *fiat* of the Annunciation expressed an abiding state of soul, extending to her whole life, and trans-
lating into action the whole theology elaborated by the
inspired teachers of Israel.

This ascendancy of God over Mary excludes from her
also all suffering which implies evil, or any interior disor-
der such as regret, remorse or scruples. Her soul is never
disturbed by those eddies and cross-currents, but is as a
clear lake. She suffered morally and physically on our ac-

count, and became the Mother of Sorrows; but that suffering was not caused by any interior lack of balance, but by the malice of men and her love for them. That same mastery of God over her which caused her to be flooded with his light removed also from her all moral or religious ignorance which might have been incompatible with her special mission. We see her wondering how the mystery of the divine motherhood is to be accomplished in her, and the reason for such a gesture on the part of God, but that region of light in which she dwells does not make the virtue of faith unnecessary in her case, though it opens up to her vistas beyond our sight. Such is the meaning of the Church's age-long teaching as regards the principal results of the Immaculate Conception, considered from what may be called a static point of view, and in its relation with the soul.

From the dynamic standpoint, her continual growth in grace has about it something prodigious. It is difficult for us to grasp the spiritual progress that is hers on account of its very rapidity, since it is comparable to that of a body falling into space, to quote St Thomas' comparison. The faster a soul rises to God, the more quickly he draws it; the greater its docility to grace, the more rapidly does it ascend to him. From the beginning, our Lady's holiness surpassed that of all the saints, and therefore her growth in grace takes place in a measure such as almost to render dizzy the mind that tries to imagine it. For that progress in sanctity is unhindered by any retrogression, any withdrawal of what has been given to God, any setback due to sin. It is a continually increasing love, an ever more ardent approach to God and an ever closer union with him.

Harmony of soul and body

Mary's body is completely in harmony with her soul. There is no sudden upsurging of the senses, no rebellion, no dallying with what is evil such as causes within us what we call concupiscence, no dualism, no disconcerting blanks. The soul reigns as sovereign over the bodily kingdom, which is exquisitely sensitive and simple. Mary's body purifies everything it meets simply by approaching it, so completely is it informed by her soul, so full is it of grace. It is a body that is perfectly docile, a living temple of the sovereign soul: such does Mary appear in the eyes of the Church. After our Lord's sacred humanity, she is the grandest triumph, the masterpiece of God. In her perfect fidelity to the order willed by the Creator, Mary shows us creation as it came from God's hands on the morning of its pristine splendour.

We shall have to return to this subject when treating of her physical integrity in childbearing, as also in connection with the Assumption, both of which illustrate in the most striking manner the harmony which has only been touched upon here.

Does this privilege exclude merit?

In order to understand how Mary could merit notwithstanding the absence of all interior opposition, it is important clearly to dissociate two ideas which to us seem closely connected: the difficulty to be overcome and the merit of the act; not that these are necessarily bound up together. So instead of beginning at ourselves, let us begin with the divine freedom.

What do we see? God is absolutely free, yet for all that he cannot choose evil; in him there is nothing whatever in the nature of struggle. The possibility of choosing evil and experiencing its fascination is, therefore, not inherent in the power to act freely. The freedom of man, whom God created in his own image, shares in the power of accomplishing the good, which is in God. Left to itself, unless it be hindered or thwarted, human freedom will be attracted towards God, and that spontaneously. The faculty of deviating from the road is not inherent in the energy of the mover, any more than the possibility of acting irrationally characterizes the reason as such. It is not essential to the first movement to hesitate, to waver, nor does it belong to a free adhesion to be able at will to turn away from what it loves. Such deviations are the consequences of a weakness, a deficiency, a wound inflicted upon the deep-seated fundamental freedom. We can scarcely understand a freedom of this quality, a freedom far superior to our own which, weighed down by the burden of our fallen and weakened nature, we find by experience to be capable of a doubtful or harmful choice.

If our darkness is to be enlightened, we must gaze resolutely upon that lightsome world where freedom is really itself. Let the soul consider the freedom of our Lord, which is absolutely beyond the reach of any assault of sin and yet remains perfect freedom. Once we have clearly grasped that fact, it will be easily understood that merit is not intrinsically bound up with the difficulty to be overcome. Were it otherwise, we should be forced to conclude that the more a soul progresses in self-control and virtue, the further it recedes as regards merit. The man who gradually conquers his passions, and in course of so doing finds it easier to act virtuously, would see his moral value diminishing instead of rising higher. The hypothesis is self-destructive.

The truth is—and this is what strikes us to the point of bewilderment—that the difficulty of overcoming an obstacle is often an invitation to redouble our generosity, to exert a superior energy and perseverance. But for us that is an accidental occasion of merit, and does not condition the value of our free acts. What matters above all regarding the moral value of those acts is not the obstacle that hinders them but the spiritual energy that clings to the good, and the strength of that inward clinging.

Mary's freedom lies entirely in the incomparable energy of her soul, which holds on to God, steadfast under all circumstances. Her life was to be the perpetual echo of the *fiat* of the Annunciation prolonged right up to Calvary. It was this unfailing steadfastness, and the vigour of this choice that never weakens, which placed in a class apart the freedom and merit of our Blessed Lady.

CHAPTER IV

DAWN:

THE ANNUNCIATION

All Mary's inward glory is but a preparation and preface for the part God has destined for her—and what a destiny! The most astounding the world has ever known: to become the Mother of God. Let us reverently read the Gospel story of the Annunciation.

When the sixth month came, God sent the angel Gabriel to a city of Galilee called Nazareth, where a virgin dwelt, betrothed to a man of David's lineage; his name was Joseph, and the virgin's name was Mary. Into her presence the angel came, and said, Hail, thou who art full of grace; the Lord is with thee; blessed art thou among women. She was much perplexed at hearing him speak so, and cast about in her mind what she was to make of such a greeting. Then the angel said to her, Mary, do not be afraid; thou hast found favour in the sight of God. And behold thou shalt conceive in thy womb, and shalt bear a son, and shalt call his name Jesus. He shall be great, and men will know him for the Son of the most High; the Lord God will give him the throne of his father David, and he shall reign over the house of Jacob eternally; his kingdom shall never have an end. But Mary said to the angel, How can that be, since I have no knowledge of man? And the angel answered her, The Holy Spirit will come upon thee, and the power of the most High will overshadow thee. Thus this holy offspring of thine shall be known for the Son of God. See, moreover, how it fares with thy cousin Elizabeth; she is old, yet she too has conceived a son; she who was reproached with barrenness is now in her sixth month, to prove that nothing can be impossible with God. And Mary said, Behold the handmaid of the Lord; let it be unto me according to thy word. And with that the angel left her. (Luke 1. 26–34.)

In order to clarify the account, we may consider it from different points of view. We may first ask ourselves what each sentence involves: what St Luke intends to convey by the expressions he has chosen: how would an ordinary young Jewess normally understand the angel's words, as the evangelist records them? This is a first scrutiny of the message as it stands. But Mary, a daughter of Israel and brought up on the Jewish scriptures, is not an ordinary young Jewess. She is Mary Immaculate, whose understanding is enlightened by reason of her privilege, whose insight is keener, hence we must inquire further. How did she, who had received all the light necessary in order to fulfil her mission, understand those deeply significant words, so decisive for her destiny? This is a second scrutiny of the message as she grasped its tremendous meaning, and both call for attention.

THE MESSAGE ITSELF

First we can examine the message in itself, and the account of the Annunciation should be read in close connection with the angel's other message foretelling the birth of St John the Baptist, for the accounts explain each other. "The Holy Spirit will come upon thee, and the power of the most High will overshadow thee." To understand them fully, we must consider them in a Biblical setting, with all the echoes they must have evoked in a Jewish girl brought up on the Old Testament.

For every believer in the old Covenant, the Holy Spirit,

the Spirit of the Lord, meant Yahweh himself. He is the same Spirit whom Isaias proclaimed would rest upon Emmanuel,[1] and who came upon other chosen persons in the Old Testament. He "wrapt them round" (with his strength).[2] He "came upon them."[3] He "filled" them.[4] That mission was temporary or permanent, according to the case, therefore it recalls what has happened previously and prepares the hearer to comprehend what follows.

"The power of the most High will overshadow thee." That power of the most High is identified with the Holy Spirit of whom mention has just been made; so it is Yahweh who will overshadow Mary. Here the perspective widens and the mystery takes on its full significance. As Fr Lyonnet, S.J., remarks in an article from which we have drawn inspiration, this overshadowing reminds us of the cloud which symbolized the veiled presence of God among the chosen people. We read in Exodus: "When all was done, a cloud covered the tabernacle, and it was filled with the brightness of the Lord's presence; nor could Moses enter the tabernacle . . . so thick the cloud that spread all about it, so radiant was the Lord's majesty; all was wrapped in cloud."[5]

As we know, the glory of God means nothing else than God himself; it was in a cloud that that glory appeared to the Jews in the wilderness, as it was in a cloud that he spoke to Moses. That cloud is mentioned again in the account of the dedication of the Temple at Jerusalem: "So the ark that bears witness of the Lord's covenant was borne by the priests to the place designed for it. . . . And with that the whole of the Lord's house was wreathed in cloud; lost in that cloud, the priests could not wait upon

---

[1] Isaias 11. 1–6 and 61. 1.
[2] Judges 6. 34.
[3] Judges 14. 19.
[4] Genesis 41. 8.
[5] Exod. 40. 32–3.

the Lord with his accustomed service; his own glory was there, filling his own house." [6] And we recognize it once more in the account of the Transfiguration on Mount Thabor: "And even as he said it, a cloud formed, overshadowing them; they saw those others disappear into the cloud, and were terrified. And a voice came from the cloud, This is my beloved Son; to him, then, listen." [7]

THE MESSAGE AS UNDERSTOOD BY MARY

Hence, she who was listening to the message must have realized that the same "glory of God" which had filled the tabernacle and the Temple was to rest upon her and in her. This was the proclamation of a mysterious feast of the dedication which would take place within her, as in a living temple. How could Mary, who better than any other understood the biblical references, fail to grasp the deep meaning of those words? Fr Lyonnet concludes:

> That divine presence which of old had hovered over the tabernacle, and so filled it that Moses was unable to enter, and had subsequently dwelt in the Temple at Jerusalem or, more strictly speaking, in the most secret sanctuary of that Temple—the Holy of Holies—that presence which was finally to consecrate the symbolical temple of the Messianic era, the angel Gabriel tells her is to become, as it were, present in her virgin womb, and to transform her into a living Holy of Holies. That divine presence which from her childhood she had been taught to venerate in one single spot on earth, there whither only the High Priest might enter and then only once a year, upon the great Day of Atonement, she learns from the angel she is now to adore within herself.

For it is indeed real adoration which is here in question. From Gabriel's words Mary learns not only of her virginal motherhood, and the Messianic character of the

[6] 2 Paral. 5. 7 and 13.
[7] Luke 9. 34–5.

Child which was to be born, but his divine character as well. Such is undoubtedly the meaning of the teaching of the ordinary and unchangeable *magisterium* of the church, and of the saints.

To be sure, the fact that the Blessed Virgin was aware of the divine sonship of her child does not imply that she possessed an elaborated knowledge expressible in formulas and concepts as later deduced by theology. Her knowledge as Mother of God was eminently intuitive and direct, and from the first she was explicitly informed of the divine identity of her Son. She was not led by some imperceptible progress, to argue from the human character to the divine. Jesus was not for her a man more or less God, whose Godhead would become more established in course of time, but from the first he was God-Man, the mystery of whom she would scrutinize with an ever-increasing veneration and a continually progressive knowledge deriving from her first initiation. If the Holy Spirit had not enlightened her concerning this fundamental fact, she would not have had the state of grace necessary for her office as Mother of God; she would not have fully realized to what she was giving her consent, and some ambiguity would have clung about the beginning of that mystery.

The Church teaches us that Mary conceived our Lord in her soul by faith before she conceived him in her womb, and marvels at that same peerless faith. Had she not understood the Godhead of her Son at the Annunciation, her faith would not only have been inadequate to the real situation, but inferior to the physical reality, since she would have engendered physically one who was the Son of God. Nay more, her faith would have been inferior to that of the Jews, who believed in the virginal birth of the Messias, while Mary, who also knew the Scriptures, knew by means of direct natural knowledge that her child was born without human intervention, and was the promised Messias.

However, the fact that she was aware of the deity of her Son in no wise excluded an ignorance as to how the messianic mission would develop. We know the incident of the finding of our Lord in the Temple at the age of twelve, and the words he addressed to his anxious parents: "Could you not tell that I must needs be in the place which belongs to my Father?" But, as St Luke adds: "These words which he spoke to them were beyond their understanding." [8] Those words prove that Mary and Joseph had not immediately understood the reason of the unexpected absence of Jesus, or how his mission was to develop, but the question he puts to them concerning "the place which belongs to" his Father—and he does not say "our" Father, and so draws attention to the fact that he is in a privileged position—emphasizes clearly and precisely that divine sonship. The said question would have been simply an enigma as far as Mary was concerned unless the Father who thus claims him had been in an altogether special and personal relationship towards him. This very question depends upon previously acquired information: on the knowledge which Mary had of her Son's divine personality. Jesus assumes it to be present and underlying her question, and his words, whatever otherwise their exegesis, make full sense only on this understanding.

Now, with the enlightening of faith, we can try to understand the theological details which make Mary's motherhood a mystery without precedent.

[8] Luke 2. 49–50.

CHAPTER V

SUNRISE:

THE INCARNATION

MOTHER OF GOD

First we can consider the doctrine of the divine mother-hood itself: "This holy offspring of thine shall be known for the Son of God." [1] Mary is the Mother of this child. In her was formed that human nature which, from the first moment of its existence, was united to the Word, the second Person of the Trinity. That child, the Word made flesh, unites indissolubly in the unity of his person, without confusion or division, the divine and human natures. It is not enough to say that Mary is the Mother of Christ, she must also be called the Mother of God. The early Christians very soon stated this point clearly. Happily, a fragment of papyrus has been found which reveals the existence in Egypt, from the third or, at the latest, the fourth century, of the antiphon still in use: *Sub tuum praesidium confugimus, Sancta Dei Genitrix:* "We fly to thy protection, O holy Mother of God." Here already we find the famous word *Theotokos* (Mother of God), the history of which is so pathetic, for concerning that title a serious controversy arose during the fifth century.

There were those who, arguing from the fact that Mary

[1] Luke 1. 35.

had not engendered the divinity of Christ but only his humanity, wished to reserve to her only the title of *Anthropotokos*—Mother of the man. The Patriarch of Constantinople, Nestorius, wishing to avoid the discussion, declared himself in favour of the formula—correct in itself—of Mother of Christ: *Christotokos,* but he meant it to be understood as a rejection of the popular *Theotokos,* and that meant that he was falling into heresy. Led by St Cyril of Alexandria, the bishops met in the Council of Ephesus, A.D. 431, and with the approval of Celestine I demanded for Mary the title of *Theotokos*—Mother of God. How enthusiastically the people of Ephesus accepted this dogmatic and irrevocable decision is well known.

When in 1931 the fifteen-hundredth anniversary of this Council was commemorated, Pius XI thus reaffirmed the Church's ancient faith: "If the son of the Blessed Virgin Mary is God, she who gave him birth rightly deserves to be called the Mother of God. If the person of Jesus Christ is one and divine, there is no doubt but that all should call Mary not only the Mother of the Man, Christ, but the Mother of God, or *Theotokos.* We all venerate her whom Elizabeth, her kinswoman, addressed as 'the Mother of my Lord' [2]: she of whom St Ignatius the Martyr said that she had 'engendered God,' and of whom, as Tertullian states, 'God was born.' "[3]

The justification of this title is quite simple. An earthly mother is such not only of the body, or the human nature, of her child, but of the actual person of that child subsisting in the body, even though God intervenes directly in the creation of the soul. Mary is not only the Mother of the body of Christ, but Mother of the Person subsisting in that body, which Person is divine, the Word of God. Nor

[2] Luke 1. 43.
[3] Encyclical *Lux Veritatis* of Dec. 25th, 1931. *Acta S.S. Pius XI,* Vol. VII.

is she the mother of a man who would be united to God, but of a man who from his conception is God in Person. It is not enough to say that Mary is mother through God's intervention: she is Mother of God, and we owe her that title under pain of failing to recognize both her Son and herself.

What must on no account be said—and we must beware of so doing—is that she is mother of the Godhead, or that she gives to our Lord his divine personality; for before ever she conceived him he *is* God from all eternity. Such is the faith of the Church, and because we are here at the heart of Christianity every exact doctrinal statement is of capital importance, and each one is a condition and motive for our adoration. Only in eternity shall we sound the depths of that *Verbum caro factum est*. We can but prayerfully ponder over it, as over a joy that can never be exhausted, as an invitation to prolong the consideration of the consequences that follow from it, as supremely the secret of Mary.

MARY, THE CHOSEN OF HER SON

This divine motherhood of Mary has features that are exclusively its own. Firstly, the mother was chosen by her Son from all eternity. It is a paradox and a unique situation and there is no limit to its consequences. Mgr Fulton Sheen expresses them well: "When God decided to become Man, he had to choose the time of his coming, the country in which he would be born, the town in which he would grow up, the nation, the race, the political and economic setting which he would inhabit, the language he would speak, the psychological conditions with which he would be in contact, as the Lord of human history and as the Saviour of the world.

"All these details would depend entirely upon one factor: the woman who would be his mother. For in choosing a mother, he would choose a social position, a language, a home town, an environment, an epoch, a destiny. His mother was not as are our mothers, whom we accept as a fact determined in history and which we cannot change. Our Lord was born of a mother chosen by him before he was born of her."

This choice implies also that *admirabile commercium*— that wonderful exchange of which the liturgy speaks. Mary confers upon the Word of God her human nature, and she does so alone, as its exclusive human source, apart from all other human intervention. Christ, the Man, is in her image and likeness; his features reflects hers, his smile, his gestures and his bearing, the accent and intonation of his voice recall those of his Mother. It is she who teaches him the language of his people and initiates him into their religious rites, the prayers, the reading of the Law, the customs and manners of his ancestors. In short, it is she who hands on to him the thousand and one details of life and behaviour which a child learns at home even without realizing it.

But in his turn the Son gives to the mother infinitely more than he receives from her. In the first place, is he not her creator—he by whom all things were made? Has he not given her even what he wills to receive from her? His human nature he takes from her because he associates his mother in the creative act, so that Creator and creature may say at the same time: "All I have is thine and all thou hast is mine." [4] Again, whereas Mary gives Jesus his humanity, he associates her with his own divine life, by an ever-increasing participation; while she forms him to her likeness, he imprints upon her soul his own divine likeness, and that far more deeply than on Veronica's veil. While Mary gives him a mortal life, he creates in her that fountain of living waters springing up to life eternal.

[4] John 17. 9.

So there is flux and reflux, reciprocal giving, and therefore the Fathers of the Church have hailed in this exchange a true marriage between God and mankind, accomplished for ever in the nuptial chamber that was
Mary's womb. Cardinal de Bérulle is only echoing tradition when he thus addressed our Lady:

> You give life to Jesus, because he is your Son, you receive
> life from Jesus, for he is your God. And thus, at the same
> time, you are both giver and receiver of life. And as the
> divine Word gives and receives at the same time, in eternity,
> being, life, and glory: receiving from the Father and giving
> to the Holy Spirit, so you, O blessed Virgin, who have the
> honour to be Mother of God: you, I say, after his example,
> and imitating him, are both a giver and a receiver of life.
> You are giving life to Christ and receiving life from him.
> You give him life, animating with your heart and mind his
> heart and mind, and you receive from the heart and body
> of him who lives and dwells in you, life in your own heart,
> your own body and your own mind all together.

VIRGINAL MOTHERHOOD

This motherhood is also different from all other motherhood because it is virginal.

The Church teaches us as a truth of faith, and not from
a mere pious sense of fitness, that Mary remained a virgin
not only after the birth of our Lord but actually in giving
him birth. This virginity in childbirth is an added delicate
touch of God's love in her regard. He willed that his
Mother should bring him forth in unalloyed joy and perfect integrity, so that to the glory of divine motherhood
would be added that of inviolate virginity. Mary knew the
happiness of bringing her child into the world while fully
aware of the mystery that was being accomplished, in a
state of closest communion with God and extraordinary
gratitude. She who when becoming the Mother of us, her
other children, would know such suffering at the foot of

the cross, brought forth her firstborn in the freshness of her maiden purity, in an ecstasy of love.

In order to understand better that divine intervention, we must see it in its relation to that other mystery of her bodily glorification, reserved for her by her Son, namely the Assumption. The latter sheds light upon the former, and this continuity leads us to repeat, with the liturgy: "O Wisdom proceeding from the mouth of the most High, reaching from end to end, mightily and sweetly disposing all things: come to teach us the way of prudence." [5] It is the same delicacy of the divine love which exempted Mary from the corruption of the tomb, which preserved her from the suffering of childbirth, showing that God loved her with an especial love that extends from the spotless soul to the pure body. The literature of the east, so sensitive to the gift of bodily incorruption, opens up a vast field for investigation to anyone wishing to study this particular aspect of the Christian religion.

Why did God will that the mother of his Son should be so privileged? But must not the birth of the Word according to the flesh recall his divine birth before all ages? Should not the Virgin's womb be in some way assimilated to the bosom of the Father and the temporal generation reflect the unspeakable purity of the eternal generation? As the Secret prayer of the Mass of September 8th expresses it; by being born of Mary our Lord did not lessen the virginity of his mother but consecrated it—*virginitatem non minuit sed sacravit*. Thus it is that faith in the Virgin-Mother and in the God-Man are so closely associated. When we proclaim that Mary is truly Mother of God, we are affirming at the same time that Christ is truly Man; when we say that he is truly God, we are on the way to understanding the integral virginity of the Blessed Virgin.

---

[5] *Magnificat* antiphon for December 17th.

The Church teaches that Mary remained a virgin before, during and after she conceived her Son. That is a dogma of faith. That she had no children after our Saviour's birth is not contradicted in the least by the expression "the brethren of the Lord" which is occasionally found in the Gospel. In Hebrew and Aramaic, the word "brother" is used in a wider sense than with us, and may equally well stand for nephews and cousins. Our Lord himself uses the word "brethren" in a wider sense still: "You have but one Master, and you are all brethren alike." [6] And elsewhere: "Here are . . . my brethren." [7] Saints Mark and Matthew call James the Less and Joseph "brethren" of Jesus,[8] and from other passages we learn that these were the sons of a certain Mary, who is clearly distinguished from the Mother of the Saviour.[9]

Even if we had not this precise language as to the extended meaning of the words "brother" and "sister" in the Bible, the account of our Lord's last moments, as left us in the fourth Gospel, would be sufficient for us. If Christ had had brothers according to the flesh, the natural course would have been for him to entrust his Mother to them before he died. Now, he does not think of James the Less or Joseph, who were commonly called his brothers. As Mary stands at the foot of the cross, he draws her attention to John, the beloved disciple, but not a member of the holy family, and says: "Woman, this is thy son." Then, turning his eyes to John, he says to him: "This is thy Mother." This clearly shows that his Mother had not had any other child to whom he would entrust the primary duty of filial love.

[6] Matt. 23. 8.
[7] Matt. 12. 49.
[8] Mark 6. 3 and Matt. 13. 55.
[9] Mark 15. 40 and Matt. 27. 56.

MOTHERHOOD IN FAITH

We must thoroughly understand what sets Mary in a place quite apart from others. For the Church, her greatness does not arise exclusively from the physiological function common to every mother; it is not the kinship of blood which matters principally although, owing to our natural tendency to include Mary in our own category, we might be tempted to think so. We might be inclined to cry with the woman in the Gospel: "Blessed is the womb that bore thee, and the breast which thou hast sucked."[10] What strikes us first is the physical birth. When, however, our Lord answers her with the words: "Shall we not say, Blessed are those who hear the word of God, and keep it?" he bids us all to see the motherhood of Mary in the light of faith. Her dignity does indeed belong to the supernatural order. She is the Mother of Christ not firstly by the flesh, but by faith. St Augustine maintains that she was happier in bearing him in her heart than in her body. She conceived her Son in her soul before she conceived him in the flesh, as the Fathers of the Church vie with one another in declaring. She gave birth to him through complete docility to the Holy Spirit who came to overshadow her.

By the *fiat* of the Annunciation, she was wholly surrendered to God, who was revealing his predilection for her, and his mighty and redeeming plans. She was the first who believed in that love which the God of mercies bears towards us, and by that act of faith Mary became the first believer of the new covenant. "Blessed are thou for thy believing," cried out Elizabeth when they met.[11] Her greatness had lain in receiving by faith the Word, the world's salvation, who was to become incarnate in her. It

[10] Luke 11. 27–8.
[11] Luke 1. 45.

is faith that lies at the origin of the divine birth and decides her attitude as a mother.

We see, therefore, how far away is the Church's teaching from the Protestant view of the Mother of our Redeemer, which looks upon her as scarcely more than the physical instrument of the Incarnation. Undoubtedly our separated brethren would agree that she has received the outstanding grace of having been chosen to be his Mother; but they do not hold that her innermost being was transformed by that grace which, as they state, leaves intact in her, as in every Christian soul, the defects caused by original sin. She carried her grace, say they, in a frail vessel, and so remained. Any other woman might have been used for the same end. A physical instrument, proper to a material function—that of giving birth to the Saviour—such is she to them: not what she is for us, namely, an instrument that is moral, conscious and free, partaking of the fullness of the mystery accomplished by means of her. They see in Mary only the meeting-place of the Creator and his creature. On their hypothesis, the divine plan for the salvation of the world would be as strange to her as the subsequent discoveries of a scholar are to the mother who brought him into the world. We see what an abyss yawns between us, and how vital it is to understand this conception in faith if we are to appreciate how truly and generously Mary cooperated in the work of salvation, and how free was her consent to the carrying out of the divine design.

IMPLICATIONS OF THIS MOTHERHOOD

This union between Mother and Son goes further than is apparent at first sight. An ordinary mother gives birth to her son, but that does not mean that she is to be his associate in his future career. She lays the first foundations of it, but is not involved in his later occupations, which will be developed apart from her. Such is not the case with Mary. By reason of her motherhood, she is involved in the work of redemption, just as the Incarnation already contains that redemption in germ. She is not the mother of someone who will one day be the Saviour and Redeemer of the world, as a priest's mother is mother of a child who will one day be called to the priesthood. It is as Redeemer and Saviour that her Son comes into the world; it is not just by accident that Jesus is the priest and victim of the New Covenant. He is born a priest and born the Lamb of God. The Greek Fathers have strongly emphasized the fact that the salvation of the world is included in the birth of Christ, and it must never be forgotten that from the first our Lady was associated in that work. From the moment of her Immaculate Conception, she was orientated towards the divine motherhood, but at the same time and *ipso facto* she was called to Calvary, since her Son, the Son of God, became incarnate in her only that he might die on the cross. The angels hovering over the manger called her Child the Saviour, the Lord and the Messias,[12] and there we have the reason why she is Mother of God; because she consents to give the world its Saviour.

As it is essential to Jesus to be born the Redeemer, so is it essential to Mary—such being the will of God—to be that Redeemer's Mother, and therefore her divine motherhood is not an accidental happening in her life, but the purpose of her existence, and the reason of her predestination and her privileges. Her motherhood is her only vocation: to bring forth her Son, and live for him is, strictly speaking, her life. In her case, St Paul's words: "For me, life means Christ," [13] are true in the fullest possible sense. Another mother can say: "This child is my life," meaning

[12] Luke 2. 11.
[13] Phill. 1. 21.

that it is her outstanding concern, but the expression is not to be taken at its face value. In Mary's case, mission and life are truly one. It is not for her own sake that she conceives her child. Her relation to the redeeming mission of her Son provides the key that enables us to understand certain words he addresses to her which seem hard to anyone who has not grasped the nature of the bond that unites them in one same apostolic preoccupation. Mary was called to enter into the silence of a transcendent mystery, and she did not refuse to accept the situation that her Son should leave her in ignorance as to how the plan of redemption would be worked out. She loved the part that was hers: that of the handmaid attentive to every expression of the Master's will, not anticipating it and not trying to find it out.

The intimacy between them had something unique in its character. It was an intimacy established in adoration, silence and unconditioned offering of herself. "The life of the Blessed Virgin," says Bérulle, "was a life of sublime adoration of the eternal Father." And in that adoration our Lord called upon his Mother to practise a faith heroic in its detachment, its total abnegation. She was the first to set out on that way of sacrifice which the Master requires all his disciples to tread. Very early on, she began by losing her Son in order to give him to us, the Son she loves with a twofold love, which is yet one: as a mother and as Mother of God.

She loves him as the best of mothers loves, but that love clings to God in a single-heartedness and a self-effacement such as we can scarcely imagine. Only the saints reveal to us in their lives something of an affection so different from our own. The love which God puts into Mary's heart for her Lord is as a devouring fire, to which her heart surrenders itself as the burning bush in the presence of *him who is*. Such a harmony is almost beyond our comprehension. It is so rare to find someone who is so passionately concerned with the interests of another as to make them his, to take them to heart more than he takes his own. In Mary, love attains to that supreme degree of fusion and identity of wills between two persons who love each other, and this we must never forget if we would understand how completely her existence is bound up with her vocation.

HISTORICAL AND MYSTICAL MOTHERHOOD

In Christ, we never dissociate the God-Man from the Head of the Mystical Body. At one and the same time, he is Son of God and Son of Mary, the Head of redeemed mankind for whom as Man he stands. Mary, likewise, because she is the Mother of Jesus Christ, the Christ of history, is also the Mother of the Mystical Body, an aspect of her motherhood which Pius XII emphasized in his Encyclical: "Mary gave miraculous birth to Christ our Lord, adorned already in her virginal womb with the dignity of Head of the Church, and so brought forth the source of all heavenly life; and it was she who presented him, the newborn Prophet, King and Priest to those of the Jews and Gentiles who first came to adore him." [14] She is the mother of the Head and the members: the former physically the latter mystically, since they are one with the Head. As St Leo says: "The generation of Christ is the origin of the Christian people, the birth of the Head is also the birth of the Body." [15] This twofold and yet one and only maternity in Mary, who engenders both the Head and the members, must be recognized. We are sons in the Son with respect to the Father as with respect to the Mother of our Saviour. In his memorable Encyclical *Ad Diem Illum,* of February 2nd, 1904, St Pius X likewise emphasized

---

[14] *Mystici Corporis*: translation made for the Catholic Truth Society, from the Latin text. See Select Bibliography at end of this volume.

[15] *Sermon* 36; Migne, *Patrologia Latina* 54. 213 (quoted hereafter as Migne, P.L.).

this dependence: "In the chaste womb of the Virgin, Christ took to himself flesh, and united to himself the spiritual body formed of those who were to believe in him. Hence Mary, bearing the Saviour within her, may also be said to have borne all those whose life was contained in the life of the Saviour. For this reason, all we who are united to Christ and, as the Apostle says, are members of his body, of his flesh and of his bones, have issued from the womb of Mary like a body united to its head. Hence, albeit in a spiritual and mystical fashion, we are all children of Mary, and she is Mother of us all: Mother, spiritually indeed, but truly Mother of the Members of Christ, which we are."

Here we are not dealing with medieval exaggerations, but with the very core of the doctrine of the Mystical Body, at the centre of true devotion to Mary. There was a time when the doctrine of the Mystical Body was somewhat shelved or neglected, and thus cut off from its roots devotion to our Lady felt the effects, so that there was a danger of its becoming sickly and sentimental. By making us share in his own attitude towards his Mother, our Lord extends his filial love for her to us who are his members. He never ceases to express this love through his brethren who have become Mary's children, so that we need have no fear that what we give to Mary is taken from him. What we give to her comes to us from him and, on the other hand, when we are of one mind with him we are responding to that very movement of his love for his Mother and, saving only the boundless love with which his Spirit inspires us for the Father and for the blessed Trinity, nothing could be more pleasing to him.

CHRIST'S FILIAL LOVE

No study of Mary's motherhood would be complete unless we tried to convey some idea of the nature of the love

of the Son for his Mother. No one was such a son as was
our Lord. His love for his Mother transcended that of all
other sons, yet there was nothing idyllic or romantic about
it. How, in any case, could he, who came not to destroy
but to fulfil the law, have failed to carry out the command-
ment he had himself given: "Honour thy father and thy
mother."

But the Son of Mary was God's own Son, and we must
never lose sight of the divine Person who, in Christ, imparts to human virtues an extraordinary depth and intensity while, at the same time, causing them to enter into the
mystery of his divine origin, and into the transcendence of
his redeeming mission. Jesus loves his Mother as no one of
the children of men has loved his mother, but that love is
exalted in its dependence on the infinite love which he
bears towards the Father who has sent him. That dependence with respect to the Father has already been shown
when he was found among the Doctors in the Temple and
answered his Mother's question with another: "Could you
not tell that I must needs be in the place that belongs to
my Father?" [16] That same attitude would never fail to
mark his entire public life.

Our Lord's filial affection was combined ineffably with
the tenderness which lies at the root of true love, and the
determination to pursue the real good of souls. A philosopher has said that love means to promote another's good,
and Christ's love was one with his will for the salvation of
all whom he loved. It was that same love which inspired
those answers to his Mother which to us seem so austere
and which found in her an echo so generous and magnani-
mous. The truth is that those replies are also addressed to
us, and are intended to teach us and to strengthen our
weakness. How many a vocation has been born from the
words just quoted! How many souls have they not helped

[16] Luke 2. 49.

to break bonds of kinship that were too human, and likely to stifle the call of God? How many have drawn from them the courage to take the decisive step?

When he spoke to Mary, our Lord was speaking to all mothers of priests, missionaries, religious of both sexes. He could rely upon her whom he has chosen to give the world its Saviour, and who lived but to make that redemption certain. May he ever meet here on earth the same faithful response from those mothers who are called to give to the Church "fishers of men!" His love for Mary stretched already beyond time and space, to all those who would share in the capacity for sacrifice and oblation of the best of mothers. Thus recognizing the magnitude of the mystery of Christ, we can give to his words and gestures a wideness of meaning that helps us to grasp their underlying significance.

CHAPTER VI

THE REDEMPTION

PASSION AND COMPASSION

The mystery of the redemption, as we have said, takes its rise from the Incarnation. Christ is born the Redeemer. Even had the Gospel not told us that Mary was present on Calvary, we should have been already aware that she was specially connected with the redemption; but, alone among the evangelists. St John expressly states that she was there. As an eye-witness, he tells the world, simply and calmly, of the suffering they shared together and the last mutual commendation of each to the other made by our Saviour. "And meanwhile his mother, and his mother's sister, Mary the wife of Cleophas, and Mary Magdalen, had taken their stand beside the cross of Jesus. And Jesus, seeing his mother there, and the disciple, too, whom he loved, standing by, said to his mother, Woman, this is thy son. Then he said to the disciple, This is thy mother. And from that hour the disciple took her into his own keeping." [1]

It is a scene poignant in its simplicity, and we need faith in order to grasp its full significance. Here we are not concerned merely with an episode, but with a culminating point in the life of our Lord and his Mother. Once, at Cana, he had said to her, "My hour is not yet come," but now his hour, which is also Mary's hour, has struck.

[1] John 19. 25–7.

It is usual for preachers to show us in those words of Christ almost exclusively a gesture of the filial love he bears towards his Mother, whom he does not wish to leave solitary and so entrusts to the beloved disciple; but when we notice that it was John who was first entrusted to Mary and not the reverse—all the more surprising since John's mother, Salome, was present on Calvary—we must conclude that this "Woman, this is thy son," goes beyond the historical person who is John. Such a manner of speaking, moreover, is typical of the fourth Gospel, replete as it is with symbolism and mystery. By order of her Son, Mary takes on the character of the new Eve, the "Mother of all living," and in the person of John the whole company of the redeemed are entrusted to her spiritual motherhood.

Let us study the text more closely. On Calvary, our Lady is both passive and active. She endures the most agonizing suffering of her life, but she also offers it to her Son and through him to the Father, in order to cooperate completely in the work of the redemption. We can now analyse this twofold aspect.

PASSIVE RÔLE

In the first place, Mary accepts the cross. Holy Scripture is silent regarding her personal agony, and not for a moment will our eyes be turned away from Christ crucified, since Mary is wholly plunged in the one mighty redeeming mystery. Her whole attention is concentrated upon God, who in Christ is reconciling himself to the world. Mary is utterly emptied of self, wholly intent upon her Son and the glory of God, fully aware of all that is at stake in the divine drama. She leaves herself out of account, as though she did not exist. Despite himself, her Son, who is her life, is causing her a state of agonizing pain, and how vulnerable did that same love for her Son render her! She lived more truly in him than she did in herself, and every blow that tortured him struck her also. Had the Father permitted it, she would have died of those mortal sufferings, and the soldier's spear that opened Christ's side pierced his Mother's soul also.

The compassion of Mary means that the very passion of our Lord is entering into her soul. The Mother surrenders herself to that divine passion while the Son associates her mental agony to his own great sacrifice. *Socia Passionis*—the companion of the Passion—the Fathers of the Church have called her. The very closeness of their union on Calvary is the final result of the permanent fusion of two loves and two lives. There is no question of setting the suffering of our Saviour and his Mother in juxtaposition. There are not two crosses prepared, but a single cross that crucifies both at the same time. Mary's cross, her share of suffering, is not, like ours, an accumulation of personal sufferings which we must unite, with more or less effort, to the cross of her Son, but, we repeat, her cross is the same cross as that of her Son. On Calvary, one, single offering unites both their hearts, making them one.

At the sacrifice of the Mass—that memorial of the passion—the priest calls upon the faithful to offer to God with him "my sacrifice which is also yours." Never was this *mine* and *yours* so perfectly realized as on Calvary, where our Lord's sacrifice was, at one and the same time, that of his Mother. A union of two lives knows here its supreme consummation; it is the seal of the covenant.

ACTIVE RÔLE

But Mary's part is not only passive. She is shown to us as the valiant woman of Scripture, standing bravely beneath the cross. *Stabat Mater,* sings the Church, and she has rebuked those who portray Mary in an attitude of one prostrated with grief, and in an attitude of collapse. The Church sees her as standing to attest her consent to Christ's sacrifice: that her will is in the most perfect accord with that of her Son who is offering himself freely to the Father —"because he willed it." Amid her anguish, Mary yet at heart retains the joy of consenting and cooperating on her part with the one sacrifice of the redemption.

What exactly is the nature of this cooperation with the redeeming act?

Let us say at the outset that if her cooperation in the sacrifice of the cross is the logical sequel of her part in the Incarnation, her situation is yet not the same in the two cases.

When at the Annunciation the angel informs her of the divine proposal, Mary stands before him representing the whole of mankind. By her acceptance she is to become the "link whereby God's greatness is united to our wretchedness," as St Francis de Sales says. Mary, who is to be our intermediary with her Son, gives us our Mediator with the Father. Therefore, once the Nativity has taken place it is her Son who will be the perfect representative of the human race, since he has deigned to take our human nature and has united it to the Godhead in the unity of his Person. On Calvary, it is Christ, not Mary, who answers for mankind to the Father, but for all that her part does not disappear. Her consent is to be found at the level of the new situation, and she offers what Christ requires of her, namely, the cooperation of the already saved humanity within her and consenting to its own redemption: the cooperation which associates the new Eve with the sacrifice of the new Adam. Before us and for us, she brings that drop of water which the priest pours into the chalice, and which symbolizes the part reserved to us: our gesture of offering which is associated with the great Sacrifice.

Our Lady's cooperation in the sacrifice of the cross has

received the particular name of *co-redemption*. Is it or is it not, fitting that she should be designated the *Co-redemptrix?* The necessity of emphasizing that Christ alone is the Redeemer in the full sense of that word has caused some theologians to hesitate at giving Mary that title, and they prefer to say that she "cooperates in the redemption" or "is associated with the Redeemer." The idea is the same, the actual name is more inclusive and direct. The majority of theologians, however, have not been put off by such fears, so evident has it seemed to them that no Catholic will mistake the meaning of the former expression. It belongs to the Church to fix the language of her theology, and to judge whether or no any confusion is likely to occur in certain cases; and in authorized documents the *magisterium* of the Church tends increasingly to favour the expression *Co-redemptrix* to express this doctrine. It has now received "the freedom of the city," so to speak, and it remains for us to explain what it involves.

By granting Mary the title of Co-redemptrix, we are not thereby withdrawing her from the world of the redeemed, and this is an important point which may well do away with hesitation or prejudice. Mary owes so much to the redeeming life and death of her divine Son that, thanks to her privilege of the Immaculate Conception, she is the first to benefit by that redemption. In her case, it took the form of an anticipated exemption: for her sake, God transscended time. On this account, she holds a place apart which will permit her subsequently, because she is the first to be redeemed, to cooperate on her own plane in the redemption of the world.

We say, "on her own plane," for we are not claiming that she can cooperate independently of the divine Redeemer, or that she can add anything to his work. Not at all! Her part is derived wholly from that of her Son, and freely integrated in his. The co-redemption must not be

understood as a collaboration on equal terms, but as a
special union with the redemption of Christ our Lord,
which is in itself plenteous—*copiosa*. Christ alone was, and
Christ alone remains, the Redeemer of mankind. It is his
blood, and his alone, that seals the reconciliation between
God and men, and all creation put together cannot add
anything to its price.

Therefore, Mary is not a cooperator in the redemption
by herself: hers is not an intrinsic sharing in the work of
atonement. It is not a contribution that adds something to
the saving action of her Son, a surplus to be coordinated
with his saving act. It is Christ himself who unites his
Mother's merits to his own, incorporates them with his
own, and offers them to God as an acceptable sacrifice. It
is certain that those merits in themselves are not on the
same level, and moreover Mary's merits draw all their
value from those of Christ and would be nothing without
the latter. Thus her co-redemption is not one of sharing
but only by loving and suffering, adhering to the infinite
redemption of Christ. In consenting, positively and ac-
tively, to the death of our Saviour, Mary is wholly plunged
into that redeeming love of her Son, and she consents in
our name as the chief and outstanding member of the Mystical Body of Christ, adhering with her whole heart to the
mystery of death and life which is being enacted before
her eyes, for her sake as for ours.

That is to say, the *fiat* of Mary on Calvary did not de-
termine the redeeming act of our Lord, did not complete
it, in no respect made its effects any greater; but her part
was willed by God as an act of full communion in the
drama of Calvary. Because such was the divine plan, in
acquiescing Mary associated us all with the one and only
restoration of all things in Christ, and with the merit of the
one Mediator. That "yes" of hers, never withdrawn since
the morning of the Annunciation, attained in the evening

of Good Friday its supreme perfection, its sorrowful and glorious fullness.

Pius XII's Encyclical on the Mystical Body expressly brings out this part of Mary at the foot of the cross:

> She it was who, immune from all sin, personal or inherited, and ever most closely united with her Son, offered him on Golgotha to the Eternal Father together with the holocaust of her maternal rights and motherly love, like a new Eve, for all the children of Adam contaminated through his unhappy fall, and thus she, who was the mother of our Head according to the flesh, became by a new title of sorrow and glory the spiritual mother of all his members. She too it was who by her most powerful intercession obtained for the newborn Church the prodigious Pentecostal outpouring of that Spirit of the divine Redeemer who had already been given on the cross. She, finally, true Queen of Martyrs, by bearing with courageous and confident heart her immense weight of sorrows, more than all Christians "filled up those things that are wanting of the sufferings of Christ for his body, which is the Church."

CHAPTER VII

MARY'S AND THE CHURCH'S MOTHERHOOD

This chapter might have been entitled "Mary and Pentecost," for in the light of that mystery all analogy between her and the Church becomes clear. In the Acts of the Apostles, St. Luke thus summarily describes for us how the little assembly in the Cenacle at Jerusalem lived after the Ascension: "All these, with one mind, gave themselves up to prayer, together with Mary the Mother of Jesus, and the rest of the women and with his brethren." [1]

The whole Church was there in that "upper room," the centre from which, as soon as they received the Holy Spirit, the Apostles set out to win the world. That house is a "high place" of prayer, and those who were praying were of one heart and one mind. It may be imagined what reverence and fervour reigned, thanks to the presence of Mary. "Home is where one starts from," an English writer has said; it is the secret source whence comes moral impetus, inspiration and energy. It was fitting that our Lady should be there in that house, with the Apostles, the centre of that group about to be transfigured by the Spirit. She to whom

[1] Acts 1. 14. As we know, these brethren were our Lord's kinsmen; St Mark (6. 3) gives their names as James, Joseph, Jude and Simon.

the angel had said of old, "The Holy Spirit will come upon thee, and the power of the most High will overshadow thee," is now waiting for the same miracle to be worked upon her children.

Is there any reason for surprise at finding Mary again present at these decisive moments? Connected as she is with the mysteries of the Nativity and the Redemption, it is but fitting that she should be present also at the birth before the world—the Epiphany—of the Church on the morning of Pentecost. The manger, Calvary, the Cenacle: those three great hours in the history of man's salvation, are naturally the greatest hours of her life on earth.

A MEETING-PLACE

The relations between Mary and the Church are becoming increasingly the subject of careful study at the present day; the question arises as soon as we consider the two equally familiar expressions, "Mary our Mother" and "Our Mother, Holy Church." Have we then two mothers, or are the two linked together by some hidden and secret bond? We cannot fail to be struck when we notice that certain texts of Scripture, especially in the Apocalypse, are interpreted by different exegetes as referring to Mary, to the Church, and sometimes to both at the same time.

This suggestion of some affinity between the two ideas, perhaps even the possibility that one is included in the other, calls for more attentive consideration. The renewal of Biblical and patristic studies had revealed treasures which, if not buried, had been at least insufficiently examined and their value not realized. We are fortunately living in days of a doctrinal exploration of the subject "Mary and the Church," which will be wholly beneficial both for further study of our Lady and for ecclesiology in general. Here is the obvious meeting-place between the

Liturgical Movement, strongly centred on the mystery of the Church, and the "Marian" movement, which has both something to receive and something to give in this matter.

There is, however, a twofold snare to be avoided: that of so immerging Mary in the Church as to fail to appreciate her unique position, and that of isolating her from the Church to such a degree as would militate against the order God has established in the realm of the supernatural. As a theologian of the present day has said in his Mariology:[2] "As Christ is reflected in Mary, so Mary is reflected in the Church . . . we can see the Church in Mary, as we can find Mary in the Church. . . . There is no contradiction involved in saying that our age is both 'an age of the Church' and 'an age of Mary.'"

To compare Mary and the Church is not easy, since each wing of the diptych, as it were, shows us many different aspects. The Church in particular can be envisaged at different epochs, if we may put it so: it existed already radically in its source of origin at the Incarnation; it was born more "formally," or explicitly, as the result of the sacrifice of Calvary, and it was officially constituted at Pentecost. And at each of these stages the mystery becomes amplified and Mary's part more diversified. But that is not yet sufficient for a fair comparison. Indeed, when we speak of the Church we may consider it as identified with Christ whom it mystically completes, or prolongs, or as distinct from him with whom it is in communion, and we prefer to choose this latter aspect. This means that Mary, whom we choose as the centre from which to make our survey, is at one and the same time "beyond" and "on this side" of the Church, so far does she surpass our logical constructions and simplifications, and so impossible is it to restrict her to our limited human analogies.

[2] Schmans, *Katholische Dogmatik,* vol. 5, p. 6. Munich, Herder, 1955.

MARY AND THE CHURCH AT THE ANNUNCIATION

Throughout her existence we see that Mary is anterior to the Church. Chronologically she precedes the historic Church, since she is already there at the dawn of the Annunciation, to consent, in the name of all mankind, to the future birth of the Church in Christ. In a certain sense, her *fiat* already contains every consent, every "yes" of the faithful of the Church in Christ. The reply, "Let it be unto me according to thy word," expresses in anticipation our partial, half-hesitating consent to the plan of salvation God has willed for us. As it were, she draws it into her own furrow and in advance covers our poor desires and half-wishes. Mary is the perfect model, the pattern according to which all the acquiescences in the will of God which are the soul of sanctity are to be modelled.

On the threshold of the New Testament, as say certain German theologians, Mary is the living symbol of the Church, which she "sums up" in her perfect fidelity. For them, she is more than a type of the Church; rather do they see her as the anticipation, even the "summit" of the Church. "The Church," they say, "makes present what was already delineated: Mary contains and represents in advance the totality of the Church, of which she is the promise and the prophecy."

AT THE NATIVITY

In the *fiat* of Mary, the Church is present. The child who is born is the Head of mankind, as of the Mystical Body. As we have said already, Mary could not conceive him physically without conceiving the Church mystically. As Mother of Christ, who unites us all, she is also Mother of the entire human race summed up in its Head, and thus Mother of the whole Church. She makes concrete this seeming paradox of being, at one and the same time, Mother of the Church because she is Mother of Christ, and daughter of the Church since her divine Son, who is Head of the Mystical Body, involves his mother in the unity of that body of which she is to be the most eminent member.

If we draw a parallel between Mary and the Church, we must say that both are mothers, not in the same sense, it is true, but both in virtue of a true motherhood.

The maternal character of our Lady stands out in a manner far surpassing every earthly analogy. We are continually tempted to apply our imagery to the supernatural world, and conceive of invisible realities in the terms of our tangible and human realities. In the same way we think of Mary's motherhood, which is the work of God, as but an inadequate image of the motherhood which we know here on earth, and at the best it is on that level that we place it. This means that we are forgetting the spiritual realities are more real than the material objects perceived by our senses. As a philosopher has put it: "The principle of identity is more solid than the floor of my room." It means that we fail to understand that heaven is more real than earth, the invisible than the visible, because the former shares more in God. So it is in the case of Mary. She is more a mother than are earthly mothers who, be they never so wonderful, are only as a shadow and reflection of her. Compared with Mary, an earthly mother is rather a nurse than a mother, so much is Mary's motherhood a unique and full source of life. It is not Mary who is a mother like our own, but our mothers who are made to her image and likeness. That is why a mother's love allows us scarcely more than an initiation into the mystery of the motherhood of our Lady; but through the love of our mothers we experience something of the love of her who is Mother of God and our mother. To alter slightly Tertullian's words, "No one is so much a father as God"—*Tam pater nemo*—we must say likewise, *Tam mater nemo*, "No one is so much a mother as Mary."

The Curé of Ars used to say that the love of all mothers put together was but as ice in comparison of the mother's love of Mary, and this is not a hyperbole, or a mere rhetorical exaggeration, but an exact statement of what there is incomparable and universal in Mary's maternity, which remains the inexhaustible source of all maternal love here in this world. And the case is the same as regards the motherhood of the Church, which reaches to depths which we can scarcely imagine. In this connection, it is well to read Bossuet's wonderful sermon on the Holy Trinity in which, addressing the Church which is the mother of all Christians, he analyses that motherhood in his usual vigorous style:

> Holy society of the faithful, Church filled with the Spirit of God, pure bride of my Saviour, in your blessed fruitfulness you represent on earth the generation of the eternal Word. God begets and you beget. He begets in himself; you give birth to your children in your womb, which is your peace, your union of hearts, your unity.
>
> Earthly mothers conceive their fruit within themselves, but once the children are born they are cast outside of the mother, whereas the Church conceives them outside of herself but gives birth to them within her. An infidel comes to the Church and asks to be taken into the fellowship of the faithful. The Church instructs and catechizes him. He is not yet within her body, within her unity. She is conceiving him, but has not yet brought him to birth. He is still outside of her, but as soon as she gives us birth we enter into her unity.
>
> Thus, Holy Church, do you beget as the Eternal Father does. For you to beget means to incorporate; to give birth to your children is not to produce them outside of you, but to make them one body with you. And as the Father in begetting his Son makes him one same God with himself, so do you make your children what you are by forming Christ

within them. And as the Father begets his Son by communication to the latter of his own being, so you give birth to your children by communicating to them that new being, which grace has given you in our Lord Jesus Christ. *Ut sint unum sicut et nos:* "That they may be one as we are one." [3]

What I say of the Father and the Son, I repeat of the Holy Spirit, who are three and yet one and the same. That is why St Augustine says: "In God there is number and yet there is no number at all. When you count the three Persons, you see a number, but when you ask what it is there is no longer a number, for the reply is that they are one and the same God. Because they are three, there is apparently a number; when you seek to learn who these persons are, the number disappears, and you no longer find anything but a simple unity." [4]

So it is with the Church. If you count the faithful, you see a number, but when you ask what the faithful are, there is no longer a number for they are all one body in our Lord. There is no longer Greek nor barbarian, Roman nor Scythian, but one single Christ, who is all in all.

MARY AND THE CHURCH ON CALVARY AND IN THE CENACLE

Mary's special position in relation to the visible Church is to be seen also from the manner in which she and the Church have a rôle in the mystery of the redemption. Both collaborate in it, but Mary, in virtue of her position as Co-redemptrix, intervenes in the actual work of reconciliation, whereas the Church does so only in the application through time and space of the salvation acquired once for all.

In the mystery of life and death, at the foot of the cross, the Church was represented in a sense in Mary. In her, the Church realized by anticipation her profound purpose, her mystery of mystical union with our Saviour. At the passion

[3] John 17. 12.
[4] *In Joan.*, tract, 39, n. 4.

Mary bore the Church in her heart, though this does not prevent our stating, equally emphatically, that on Calvary Mary was in the Church, as the first member of it to be redeemed by the sacrifice of her Son: redeemed by anticipation, the most eminent member of that "people God means to have for himself," whom he acquired at the price of his blood (I John 2. 9).

If we compare Mary and the Church from the point of view of the mystery of Pentecost, the perspective is altered, because this time the Church is seen in the full light of day, with its hierarchic constitution functioning. In this hierarchic, visible, structural, sacramental element of the Church, Mary has no part. From this standpoint of historical reality, it is henceforth the society built upon Peter, on the Twelve endowed with the powers of its *magisterium,* its ministry and its government. Mary remained among the faithful who benefit from this divine society. For that reason, in view of avoiding any possible confusion, the Church finally forbade the title of "the Virgin-Priest," which some wished to give to Mary. However, in order to react against the above notion it would not be right to put Mary in a state of inferiority in relation to the priest.

Some people insist upon the fact that Mary is incapable of consecrating or absolving, as though on that account she is completely disassociated from the priesthood; but that is to forget that, although not herself possessing the priestly character, she is the mother of the great High Priest, from whom all priesthood is derived. Consequently, without herself carrying out any priestly functions, she surpasses in dignity all earthly priests. We cannot validly compare Mary and the priest if we forget the preponderant part she has had even in the formation of Christ's priesthood, which was brought about in her by the Holy Spirit when that same Spirit united our Lord's sacred Humanity to His Godhead.

Mary does not enter directly into the sacramental economy: it is not she who gives to the sacraments the power proper to them, that is, the power which permits their acting immediately upon souls for the latter's sanctification; but she intervenes indirectly in their saving action by inclining the hearts of her children towards the moral dispositions required by the sacraments if the latter are to bestow their grace effectively.

The sacraments do not act automatically, but must find favourable dispositions in those who receive them. They bear fruit in us only if we receive them confidently in faith and if our wills are upright. Mary's part is to open our hearts, inspiring us with desires to be pure, to be ever at God's disposal and to await his coming full of hope. Mary does her part in what theologians call the human cooperation, *ex opere operatis,* in the sacramental action. What she does not do visibly and tangibly, she brings to pass in her own motherly way, which is wholly of persuasion, in human hearts and consciences. She takes us into the mystery of communion with our Lord wherein her sanctity is fully displayed. We must not forget that these two aspects of the Church, visible and invisible, are complementary, as Pius XII so urgently reminds us. They must be distinguished one from the other, but only in order that they may be the better united, lest we oppose a visible to an invisible Church, which would mean the very negation of the divine plan.

DEVOTION TO MARY AND TO THE CHURCH

It follows that if we are willing to enter into the divine purpose and abide there, devotion to Mary necessarily means devotion to the Church. It is nonsense to love Mary and not love the Church. To love Mary means precisely *sentire cum Ecclesia,* as theologians express it, that is, to be entirely of one mind with the Church, and to enter into that stream of grace that flows from her. It is impossible to conceive of piety towards Mary that is something apart from that we bear towards the Church, that, so to say, is not always coming back to the Church. A spirituality that is deeply rooted in the Church cannot be nourished on private revelations, or expressed only by particular pious practices. Such piety would be depriving itself of the lights of divine Revelation, as also of the strength derived from the great streams of devotion that flow from the Church and carry it on to Mary.

Not that this implies excluding all popular devotion, for example, but it does imply a sense of proportion and measure. We have no right to put on the same level any revelations, imposed upon us only on the plane of human prudence and appealing only to human credibility, with the divine revelation which was closed at the death of the last Apostle, and requires us to believe with theological faith.

What is true with respect to piety in the restricted sense is true also as regards our behaviour towards the Church. Our piety towards our Lady causes us to enter into the mystery of her motherhood of grace, and that is exercised only in and by the Church. The ministry of the priesthood makes use of the benefit of Mary's spiritual maternity in order to make fertile the actual maternity of the Church. We can see how these two complete each other.

This motherhood of grace in Mary, and in the Church with and by Mary, corresponds to the outpouring of the incomparable fatherhood of God. It is the channel whereby we come into contact with "that Father from whom all fatherhood in heaven and on earth takes its title" (Ephes. 3. 15). That fatherhood of God includes in the

fullness of its simplicity the very perfection of motherhood. Unlike what prevails on earth, in God there is no
dualism; he bears in himself all fruitfulness. The Father's
love is unique and a love of plenitude, and Scripture sees
fit to express it in terms of a mother's tenderness: "Can a
woman forget her child? . . . Let her forget; I will not be
forgetful of thee" (Isaias 49. 15). The Church inherits
that fruitfulness and that tenderness. She has received it
from the Father by Mary, who gave the world Jesus
Christ, who was truly the Father's Son, and with him the
life of grace. Exercised among men by means of the
priestly ministry, that motherhood of the Church is indeed
the very fatherhood of God in operation.

FATHERHOOD IN THE PAPACY

We are too prone to think of the Church with her constituted hierarchy as an administrative institution with its
fixed departments, laws and jurisprudence, without dis-
covering at the heart of this structure, which is necessary
just as some organization is necessary to every visible society, the reality of the grace which animates it.

No one better than Mary can help us to love "holy
Mother Church," to understand the mystery of her
motherhood, that motherhood which shares so intimately
in the divine fatherhood as does the motherhood of Mary
herself whence it takes its roots.

In the light of faith the supreme Head of the Church is
not only, or primarily, the Sovereign Pontiff who holds the
power of the keys, but the father of Christendom—the
"Holy Father." The title "Pope" calls up nothing else than
that fatherhood whence all his authority is derived. In his
eyes, the faithful are not first and foremost servants who
obey, but children. If they kiss his ring, it is not merely to
conform to etiquette, but as a filial gesture. If they bow to

his authority, it is because they know that the primacy is a prerogative of service and of love. First and foremost he is the "common Father" of the faithful, who distributes to them the bread of the word of God and the lifegiving sacraments.

Beneath the cupola of St Peter's runs an inscription that sums up what Rome means for each member of the Church: *Hinc unitas sacerdotii exoritur:* "From here the unity of the priesthood takes its rise." It might be paraphrased: "Here originates the highest earthly fatherhood." Since Mary has been given charge of the birth and growth of the Christ-life in souls, she renders possible the highest spiritual fatherhood; she enables the Head of the Church, the Church herself, to bring forth children unto grace, to communicate light and life.

FATHERHOOD IN THE EPISCOPATE

A further mystery of paternity is to be found in every bishop whom the Holy Spirit has entrusted with a portion of the Church. "You may have ten thousand schoolmasters in Christ, but not more than one father; it was I who begot you in Jesus Christ" (I Cor. 4. 15). Every bishop can take these words as addressed to himself, then to his priests and people. St Ignatius of Antioch did not hesitate to write: "It is the very power of God the Father which you should venerate in your bishops," and elsewhere he calls the bishop "the image of the Father." Moreover, it is this conception of which the Church reminds the bishops when dictating to them their rule of conduct: "Let them remember that they are shepherds of souls: that they must rule their subjects not in order to tyrannize over them, but to love them as sons and brethren."

The world is tempted to see in a bishop a sort of ecclesiastical governor or overseer, whose duty is to promulgate laws and decrees and undertake the general supervision of the local Church. He is regarded from the point of view of his human qualities, and more often than not is seen as an adversary, and his actions interpreted from a political standpoint. The world which does not understand the things of God—and unfortunately too many Catholics belong to the world as regards this matter—is unaware of that spiritual fatherhood which is the soul of the episcopate. It may happen that, owing to force of circumstances, such as the size of the flock and the many duties involved, this fatherly character becomes overshadowed and rendered less proximate and direct in individual cases; that is the price paid for what is no longer on a human scale. But faith must rise above these contingencies, as also above the human weaknesses of individuals, and since all carry their treasures in frail earthen vessels, our attention must be directed rather to this mystery of fatherhood which is at work in the bishop.

It is he who is at the source of the priesthood in his particular portion of God's Church. A man is not ordained priest without being attached to a diocese, and every priest is necessarily a collaborator of the bishop. It is the bishop who concelebrates his first Mass with him; the church of which he is put in charge has been consecrated by the bishop; the altar and chalice have been anointed by him. The word of God which the young priest transmits will be a participation in the authentic teaching of his bishop, just as his powers of jurisdiction are derived from the same source. It is one same wave which from the original spring feeds each stream, and it is in the unity of this mystery of life that the Church draws her strength and her continuity.

Thus, then, the fatherhood of the pope, like that of the bishops, is a reflection of the spiritual motherhood of Mary; our filial attachment towards both is the normal result of all true devotion to her.

CHAPTER VIII

THE ASSUMPTION

On the feast of All Saints, 1950, Pius XII proclaimed as a dogma of faith *urbi et orbi*—"to the City and to the world" —the Assumption of the Blessed Virgin.

"We define that it is a dogma divinely revealed that Mary, the Immaculate Mother of God, ever a virgin, at the end of the course of her earthly life was raised with her body and soul to heavenly glory."

Every word matters. In this intensely concentrated passage the Pope alludes to the Immaculate Conception, the divine motherhood, and the perpetual virginity of our Lady. These are the three truths of faith which, as their logical completion, call for the dogma of the Assumption.

Without seeing therein an absolute requirement, it seems highly fitting that the first victory of Mary over Satan should be perfected by a victory over death. She was conceived without sin, so she will escape death which is the consequence of the revolt against God which is sin. By sin, death entered into the world, and the wages of sin is death. Christ's victory will be complete when death has been destroyed. "We ourselves, although we have already begun to reap our spiritual harvest, groan in our hearts, waiting for that adoption which is the ransoming of our bodies from their slavery" (Rom. 8. 23). Again, St Paul says: "We find our true home in heaven. It is to heaven that we look expectantly for the coming of our Lord Jesus

Christ to save us: he will form this humbled body of ours anew, moulding it into the image of his glorified body" (Phil. 3. 20–1). That means that our redemption is not finally achieved: that we are still partially vanquished, that "saved in hope" we still bear the trace of the curse pronounced against Adam, so long as our bodies are not yet glorified. As a result of the Immaculate Conception, the devil had never any hold upon our Lady, and from that initial exemption it follows that she should also be granted an anticipated glorification. The Assumption is the logical consequence of the Immaculate Conception—a logic immanent in one same love. It completes the victory formerly begun by an anticipated liberation, and the final mystery is correlative to the initial mystery.

DIVINE MOTHERHOOD AND THE ASSUMPTION

In this context, Pius XII mentions the title of Mother of God. In the Bull *Munificentissimus Deus,* proclaiming the dogma, he speaks explicitly of the close bond uniting Mother and Son. Filial love, like maternal love, is rooted in the depths of the body as in those of the soul, and we can understand that in our Lord's love for his Mother he willed for her this bodily glorification. For Mary, the Assumption means that suddenly, with her human eyes, she sees again her Son and God; it means the embrace of the Child welcoming his Mother into his arms. Long before the doctrine was proclaimed, Christian instinct felt that this gesture towards her who gave him his humanity was one becoming the Word made flesh. Christendom saw it as following naturally upon the Incarnation itself. An Anglican theologian, the late E. C. Rich, who was received into the Church in 1956, has related how troubled he was when he learnt that the Assumption was to be defined, because he could not discover any trace of such a dogma in

Scripture, and he has thus movingly described how the light came into his soul.

"On Whitsunday, as I was kneeling at the altar to receive Holy Communion (that is in the Anglican church), when I was not thinking in the least about the Assumption, or of my religious doubts, but was, on the contrary, absorbed in the thought of the sacrament, all at once, the words "This is my Body" shone before me so strongly and clearly that I understood the whole unity of the Catholic Faith, including the place held by Mary and by her Assumption. I realized how faith in the Immaculate Conception, and now in the Assumption, had arisen in the hearts and minds of the faithful whilst they adored and pondered upon the mystery of the Incarnation." [1]

That discovery led him to the Catholic Church.

Finally, the pope alludes to Mary's perpetual virginity. As we said when establishing the Church's belief in the bodily integrity of our Lady before, during and after childbirth, this same faith is completed here by recognizing her bodily glorification. The dogma of the resurrection of the body is an integral portion of the Creed: the Church has drawn from it her respect for the body as the temple of the Holy Spirit. The Assumption, an anticipation of the resurrection of Mary, enters into the same perspective, and reveals the same delicate fittingness. We are not saying that the fact that it is so highly fitting suffices of itself to justify the doctrine, but it does shed light upon the living tradition of the Church which, in the course of ages, has lived this truth before defining it; and shows how greatly that tradition has been enriched and supported by the many corroborative elements of the faith, as the volume of a river is increased from the tributaries that flow into it.

[1] See the London *Catholic Herald*, May 25th, 1956.

THE ASSUMPTION WITH RESPECT TO CHRIST

The Assumption is not an ascension. Christ alone raised himself to heaven by his own power. Mary is raised thither by the power of another: drawn there passively by the divine power, as a soul is raised in an ecstasy. When we celebrate this feast, we are honouring the victory of our Lord himself, the final triumph of the gratuitous love of God; for Mary rises to heaven drawn thither by her Son, and thus sharing in "the power of his resurrection," [2] attesting in her own body, that her Son has vanquished death on the morning of Easter Day, and that our most daring hopes are well and truly founded. If Christ himself is the pledge of our future resurrection, the glorious vision of Mary in her Assumption brings us a foretaste of the former.

THE ASSUMPTION WITH RESPECT TO MARY

If we consider the effects of this mystery in Mary herself, we see that there is about it a supreme "balance"; the Assumption effects a complete harmony. In her the body is perfectly docile to the soul, and the soul is completely in the hands of God. In her, his kingdom is established "on earth as it is in heaven"; on an earth that has become heaven, as far as it is possible for a human being to be thus merged with the world above.

In Mary assumed into heaven, the perfect spiritual order has been accomplished. The soul rules the body, causing it, as it were, to vibrate, as the harpist touches the strings of his instrument as he will and draws forth the most delicate tones. In her, what is exterior faithfully reflects what is within. Her whole outward being is like a stained-glass window, glowing in the light of the divine

[2] Phil. 3. 10.

sun: "All the glory of the king's daughter is within," [3] says Holy Scripture, and that is true as far as Mary's earthly life was concerned; but now that beauty shines forth radiant, for the joy of Paradise. In her, the promises of the Beatitudes suddenly appear, as the flowers in spring burst forth from the opening buds. It is well to re-read the Sermon on the Mount in the light of its realization in the Mother of God.

> Blessed are the poor in spirit; the kingdom of heaven is theirs.
> Blessed are the patient; they shall inherit the land.
> Blessed are those who mourn; they shall be comforted.
> Blessed are those who hunger and thirst for holiness; they shall have their fill.
> Blessed are the merciful; they shall obtain mercy.
> Blessed are the clean of heart; they shall see God.
> Blessed are the peace-makers; they shall be counted the children of God.
> Blessed are those who suffer persecution in the cause of right; the kingdom of heaven is theirs.

Mary shares in each of those Beatitudes, and in a supreme degree they are fulfilled in her. Not in vain did she prophesy in her *Magnificat:* "Behold from this day forward all generations will count me blessed," and not in vain do the faithful greet her, as did Elizabeth, as "blessed among women." That kingdom of heaven, that earth to be received as a heritage, that limitless domain of joy, justice, mercy, and that blessed vision of peace, Mary enters as a Queen and as her right.

Because she was poor, divested of self as she was of earthly riches: because she was the lowly handmaid of the Lord, who found grace with him: because she was the Mother of Sorrows, to whom the Church applies the lament of Jeremias: "Look well, you that pass by, and say if there was ever grief like this grief of mine. . . . Might

[3] Psalm 44. 14 (Vulgate and Douay version).

I but confront thee with such another as thyself! What
queen so unhappy as Jerusalem, what maid as Sion deso-
late? How can I comfort thee? Sea-deep is thy ruin, and
past all cure." [4] Because she willed only that fulfilment of
God's justice, which is but one and the same with his love:
because she was the Mother of Mercy, who forgave the
Apostles their desertion of her Son, Peter his denial, the
executioners their deicide.

Because she was Immaculate, clean of heart, one upon
whom the devil had never the slightest hold, and who
purifies everything she touches. Because she was the en-
voy of peace between heaven and earth, and opened the
era of the new and eternal covenant: because, on account
of her Son, she was as a sign of contradiction, from the
massacre of the Innocents to the descent from the cross.

SPIRITUAL MOTHERHOOD AND QUEENSHIP

The Assumption is an investiture, and from it the
motherhood of grace receives its consecration. At the Incarnation, because Jesus became the Head of the human
race, Mary became the mother of men. On Calvary, our
Saviour himself proclaimed that motherhood: "This is thy
mother," and at Pentecost the newly born Church sees
Mary carrying out her office with respect to the Apostles
and the first faithful. At the Assumption, her motherhood
attained its full efficacy; its benefits become universal, and
she becomes Mediatrix with the Mediator.

She receives power to look upon us, each and all, with
a mother's watchfulness. Lost in God by means of the beatific vision, she yet knows us, one by one, by name, and
knows the whole story of each one's life. When she uttered
her *Fiat* at Nazareth and again on Calvary, she conceived
us all and gave us birth, but collectively. Henceforth in

[4] Lam. 1. 12 and 2. 13.

heaven she acts upon us more individually. It is by being plunged in God, and without ceasing to gaze upon him, that Mary bends over us, follows us step by step, knows our smallest needs. Did not our Lord say of the angels appointed to be the guardians of the children of men that they "behold the face of my heavenly Father continually"? [5] It is there, in the face-to-face vision of God, that they reach us better than anywhere else, for in God they attain the very source of our being.

Still more than the angels, owing to her motherhood, is Mary immersed in the vision of God as in an ocean; there she views the whole world. No movement of coming and going withdraws her from God so that she may come to us, as we have to leave prayer in order to give ourselves to work. She remains fixed in God, and that rest is her activity, her prayer is intercession, her ecstasy, mediation, her contemplation, incessant action.

In the glory of her Assumption we have no difficulty in understanding the Queenship of Mary with respect to the world, which Pius XII proclaimed when instituting the liturgical feast of Our Lady, Queen of the World, to be kept on May 31st. The Church's tradition, whether in pontifical documents or in the liturgy and in art, greets Mary as the Queen of all creatures, Queen of the world, Sovereign of the Universe.

As Pius XII wrote: "The principal argument upon which Mary's royal dignity is based . . . is beyond all doubt her divine motherhood. In fact, it is stated in the Scriptures of the Son to be born of the Virgin: . . . 'Men will know him for the Son of the most High; the Lord God will give him the throne of his father David, and he shall reign over the house of Jacob eternally; his kingdom shall never have an end.' [6] Moreover, Mary is declared 'the

[5] Matt. 18. 10.
[6] Luke 1. 32 and 38.

Mother of the Lord.' It follows logically that she herself is a queen, since she has given life to a Son who from the moment of his conception, even as Man, was on account of the hypostatic union of his human nature with the Word, 'King and Lord of all.' "

But Pius XII appeals further to the part played by Mary as Co-redemptrix of mankind. "There is no doubt that only Jesus Christ, God and Man, is King in the full, correct, absolute sense of the word; but, all the same, Mary shares also in that royal dignity although by analogy and in a limited degree; for she is the Mother of Christ who is God, and associated with the work of the divine Redeemer in his struggle against his enemies and in the triumph which he has obtained over them all. In fact, through this union with Christ the King, she attains to a glory so sublime that it surpasses in excellence all created things. From this same union with him, flows the royal power that authorizes her to distribute the treasures of his kingdom, and finally it is the unfailing source of the inexhaustible efficacy of her mother's intercession with the Son and with the Father."

In honouring the queenly dignity of Mary, the Church is merely making explicit in the liturgy a veneration proclaimed a thousand times. In a century when men are becoming increasingly aware of the dimensions of the world, the Church wills to show Mary as Queen of a universe which, however wide it may be, remains enveloped in the folds of her mantle.

THE ASSUMPTION AND ITS PROCLAMATION AT THE PRESENT TIME

Not only does the Holy Spirit guide the Church in order to introduce her into the fullness of truth, and preserve her from deviating therefrom, but he intervenes also to choose the hour and moment of that progressive knowledge. The

Master had told his disciples that there were truths which they could not then comprehend and which would be shown them subsequently. All through the Gospel we can trace, as it were, a divine "jealousy" in reserving to himself the choice of his hour and not allowing anyone to anticipate it. Such is the law of Providence. Scripture tells us that God hears us at the time marked out by him.[7] It is the same as regards the hour and the century which he chooses in order to manifest his name to men more clearly. If the Holy Spirit has reserved to the middle of the twentieth century the proclamation of the dogma of the Assumption, that choice corresponds to some mysterious reason which we are not forbidden to scrutinize.

CHRISTIAN RESPECT FOR THE BODY

Undoubtedly, one of the reasons is to remind the world of today of the sacredness of the human body. When we see how far the Church carries her respect for the body, and the motherly care with which she surrounds it, we cannot but be impressed. No philosophy, no religion, except Christianity, has attached to the body so lasting a significance and promised it so glorious a future. Materialists even teach unanimously that bodily corruption is the end of everything, and Communism, which is the most modern expression of materialism, stands for a doctrine of dissolution and annihilation of man after death.

The proclamation of the doctrine of the Assumption has recently been inscribed in the historical record of the twentieth century as a challenge to this contemporary materialism, which began with "the death of God," spoken of by Nietzsche, and which, as we see before our eyes, leads to the death of man who is reduced to nothingness. At the same time the doctrine is also a safeguard in deny-

[7] 2 Cor. 6. 2.

ing all sublimation of man which tears him away from his human nature and rejects his incarnate reality.

On the contrary, the Church has always taken the part of man's human condition, and she will have nothing to do with a spirituality which considers the body as the prison of the soul. She believes in the unity of man: that unity which modern psychology is bringing out more and more clearly. Her care is not only for the soul but for the human person in its total reality. Christ is not only the life of the soul but the life of the man. It is the whole that comes first, not the parts. Man is not a soul and a body, or a soul clothed with a body, but a living body and a soul *incarnated* in it. A man does not possess a soul as he possesses a car, nor is his body an annex of the soul, but at one and the same time he is his soul and his body. Never for one moment does the Church forget that, and she defends the unity of the composite human being against all deviations from that truth. Against the gnosis which identified the body with evil and attributed its creation to an evil principle, a doctrine which led its adherents to prohibit marriage as being a sin, the Church proclaimed her faith in the "Creator of all things, visible and invisible."

If she defends the excellence of the vocation to virginity, she praises without circumlocution the sacred character of marriage, and the reverence due to the latter. St Thomas does not hesitate to declare that original sin has not changed the fundamental nature of the procreative act, and that before the Fall, since all concupiscence would have been absent, that act would have found a more perfect echo in a more sensitive and better ordered body.[8] The Church likewise fought the Jansenism which declared war upon human sensitiveness and natural human values, on the pretext that original sin had corrupted man to the very marrow. She condemned Jansenism, and re-

[8] *Summa Theol.* Supp. Pars III, Q. 42, a. 1–3.

fused to undervalue man in order to exalt a supernatural-
ism "in the clouds." We see there an unvarying feature
of her theology as regards man, as also of her everyday
dealings with him. We need only watch her in action.
Every morning before communicating, the priest adores
the Blessed Sacrament as "a safeguard of both soul and
body"; every prayer of her ritual proclaims this respect
for the body, whether it be a question of administering Extreme Unction to the gravely sick, or of funeral rites,
whether sacraments or sacramentals are concerned. The
Church blesses the lowliest objects; bread and water, wine
and oil, fire and fruits, seeds and crops, houses and marriage beds. For her, the whole man is sacred, and everything can be for him a means of grace.

The Assumption is, as it were, a shortened instruction
on our last end, an illustration which confirms this realism
of the Church. We know that of itself the soul is immor-
tal and survives without the body, and that before the
resurrection it experiences the joy of the beatific vision; but
the Assumption of our Lady reminds us that if the substance of this joy cannot know any increase, it will know a
corporal "resonance," an added splendour in the flesh,
once the resurrection, whether accomplished at the last
day, as with us, or anticipated as in Mary, has taken
place.[9]

Moreover, if man is a unity, is it not normal that the
glorification of the soul should involve that of the body,
and lead to the complete triumph of the glorified Christ in
himself and in us? We must repeat: it is sin, and not matter as such, which has brought about the disequilibrium
in man and ultimately caused death. At the resurrection,

[9] A theological opinion, which is being increasingly held, admits
that at the resurrection of the body there will be an increase of
the intensity of the soul's happiness. Such, at least at one time,
was the opinion of St Thomas (*Summa Theol.* Pars III, Supp., Q.
75, art. 1–2.

the body will espouse the soul with a facility equal to its strength. Like the angels in Dante who receive a crown the colour of each one's hair, so will the body receive that appropriate glory, its due measure of salvation. It will be the glorious body of a glorified soul, and the new properties of that body will be none other than the sensible reception of the spiritual properties that are requisite: the obedience of the matter which is at last enfranchised. And that is the triumph which in Mary's case is anticipated as a pledge and a hope for us.

We can understand how in this world of darkness in which we live, the dogma of the Assumption breaks forth like the northern lights, and repeats this message to us in a more telling manner than ever; we must not despair of man and we must believe in the actuality of our Lord's resurrection and the resurrection of the body. It brings to us the echo of the joy of Easter, so wonderfully sung by St Augustine in his *Commentary on the Psalms:* "From whence shouldst thou believe unless an example of flesh assumed from the mass of thy death went before? Therefore in him first we have risen again. . . . Christ rose again, as thou art to rise. . . . Thou didst fear death; he died: thou didst despair of rising again. . . . But he rose again in that which for thee he received of thee. Therefore thy nature in him hath preceded thee. . . . Therefore he ascended first and we in him, because that flesh is of the human race." [10]

THE ASSUMPTION AND SATAN

The Assumption has yet another valuable significance at the present day. It celebrates the victory of Christ over evil and particularly over Satan. In order to form an idea of the measure of the struggle, we must return in thought

[10] *In Psalmos,* Sermo 2. 10; Migne, *P.L.* 36. 899.

to the origin of society. The devil comes in order to lead the father of our race into temptation, and inaugurate here on earth his reign as Prince of Darkness. In that sorrowful night, a light is lighted and a prophecy shines forth "like a lamp in some darkened room, until the dawn breaks, and the daystar rises in your hearts." [11] That brightness is written in letters of fire in God's promise that the enemy shall be crushed: "I will establish a feud between thee and the woman, between thy offspring and hers; she is to crush thy head, whilst thou dost lie in ambush at her heels." [12] Mary is the only creature in whom Satan's power was completely overcome and over whose soul and body he has never any hold. That is enough to mark her place at the centre of the world's history, for it is impossible to comprehend that history, nor its tragic, and sometimes infernal, character, unless we take account of the dark machinations of him who was the Father of lies and a murderer from the beginning.

Anaemic as we have become, we find it hard to believe in the powers of evil in a realistic way, in those accursed "spirits of darkness who wander in the world for the ruin of souls," as Leo XIII expressed it.[13] Yet for all that St Paul is constantly reminding us: "It is not against flesh and blood that we enter the lists; we have to do with princedoms and powers, with those who have mastery of the world in these dark days, with malign influences in an order higher than ours." [14]

We have been duly warned as to the existence and activity against the Church, which is the kingdom of God on earth, and another kingdom which stands against it; and it is not for nothing that the Church prays that her

[11] 2 Peter 1. 19.
[12] Gen. 3. 15.
[13] Prayer to St Michael said after low Masses.
[14] Ephes. 6. 12.

children may be given "grace to avoid all contact with the evil one, and with a pure mind to serve thee, the only God." [15] If, in their simplicity, our ancestors sometimes overstressed this demoniacal presence, we have gone to the opposite extreme, and no longer recognize, under his many disguises, him who is the direct instigator or the accessory of all the sins and crimes of mankind. It is Mary who leads the armies of God, Mary who "in battle array so awes men's hearts," who crushes the serpent's head, and whom he dreads above all others, because to her God has entrusted his own sword, and there is no better fighter than a mother, when the issue is the lives of her children.

THE ASSUMPTION AND THE PAROUSIA

The Assumption also draws the attention of the faithful to the Church triumphant of the end of time, to the Parousia. Fr Bouyer has called Mary "the eschatological icon of the Church." Mary, he says, offers at the birth of the Church, as though summed up in one person, the same perfection which at the end of time is to reach its full development in a multitude of believers, gathered together in one. She is the symbol and the pledge of Catholic unity.[16]

Mary, glorified, calls upon us also to long for that final term, that glorious return of our Lord. There is in the Church a constant impetus towards that kingdom which is to come and shall have no end. We are travellers, Mary has arrived. She helps us to live "until he comes," at that coming that changes into relatives all our earthly absolutes. She obliges us to walk with eyes fixed upon heaven, whither she has gone before us and now awaits us. She

---

[15] Collect for the 17th Sunday after Pentecost.
[16] *Le culte de la Mère de Dieu, Irenikon*, 1949, XXII, pp. 150 and 156.

whispers into the Christian's ear that supreme prayer with which Holy Scripture closes: "Come, Lord Jesus!" *Veni Domine Jesu!* In those words is expressed the whole yearning of her own soul between the day of Pentecost and the Assumption: the very breath of her life. She urgently exhorts us to live, already here on earth, the life of heaven, and to familiarize ourselves with that world which is at once so near and so far; so near because it is already within us, and so far because we are continually forgetting it and understand it so imperfectly.

The Assumption is a glimpse of heaven, the lifting of a veil hiding another world, an encouragement to make our faith something concrete. We are so prone to prefer the tangible here on earth to "the shadows of the beyond," and to think of heaven, as did the Jew and the Greek, as a joyless kingdom of "unreal" spirits. Is it at all astonishing then that we are tempted to prefer the shadow to the substance, today rather than tomorrow, and if we fail in practice to reconcile the two duties, equally imperious, of being citizens of the world and aspirants to heaven? We do not *really* hope for that eternal life of which our prayers speaks except as late as possible!

How, again, can the vision of heaven stimulate us if the picture of it which we have in mind is bereft of all human movement, and so rarified and ethereal that it is something alien from all our earthly values? Is heaven a solitude, a negation of everything which the soul has known and loved? It is striking to notice how great poets who have treated of the world beyond, such as Milton and Dante, become so reserved when they reach the last stage of their journey to Paradise: when they call upon us to contemplate "three coloured circles of equal form." That symbol of the Trinity will seem very far away and unreal to the ordinary reader, who will see in heaven only an artificial, airless region, a *sheol* lacking all vitality. Will everything, then, be silence and desert before the majesty of God?

The Assumption offers us another picture of heaven. It shows on the right hand of the risen Christ, the Queen of heaven, glorified in her body as in her soul. Therefore heaven ceases to be something "disincarnate" thenceforth, for with Christ and his Mother, earth has in a way entered into heaven. In them, we find already that "new heaven and new earth," of which the Apocalypse tells us. In them, it is humanity, made of our flesh and blood, which enters into heaven and there creates a family atmosphere, that of a home as we understand it. Their presence bears witness that if grace does not destroy nature but perfects it, glory in its turn exalts nature whilst surpassing it. As the human race contemplates its glorified Mother, it begins to suspect something of that which eye hath not seen, nor ear heard, or the human mind been able to grasp, but which God has prepared for those who love him. In Mary, it greets the success of God's creation, which integrates and makes eternal all values; in her it sees the sacring of our human condition.

How can we fail to wish that preachers of the present day would lay more stress upon the riches of heaven: upon that symphony of light and joy, and teach our contemporaries to contemplate and savour the things beyond with a really living faith! The proclamation of the dogma of the Assumption is an urgent summons to be bolder in introducing the faithful to the splendour of God.

CHAPTER IX

MARIA MEDIATRIX

ACQUISITION AND DISTRIBUTION
OF GRACES

The mediation of Christ is to be studied in three phases. From the first, the Incarnation constitutes him the Mediator, because in his person are united the two extremes to be reconciled, God and man. In the second phase, the sacrifice of the cross, the mediation is carried out in fact, since thereby God and man are reconciled. The third phase, which is the application to mankind of the redemption that has been acquired, is merely the working out through the ages of the second phase.

Mary intervenes at each of these stages. We have shown how she cooperates at the Incarnation and the Redemption, and it remains to define the nature of this cooperation not now as regards the acquisition of graces but in their distribution. *A priori,* we should expect to find Mary again at this final stage and see her taking a part coextensive with the mystery of Christ. Moreover, this part is all the more easily understood in that the present phase has its roots deep in the past and brings us the benefit thereof.

We can and should distinguish the acquisition of the redeeming merits which belongs to the past, since the redemption was won on the evening of Good Friday, and the application of those same merits which takes place today throughout time. This application is not something additional, as would be the epilogue of a book that is complete in itself, nor is it the making present of the past. In the fifth century, already this continuity was admirably explained by St Caesarius of Arles, when he wrote: "Every day the tireless redemption continues to save mankind." The redemption applied is still truly the redemption.

Hence it is to be expected that our Lady's mediation should not be restricted to her past cooperation in the redemption, but should extend also to the redemption in the present and make actual and individual the salvation won by the blood of the Redeemer. Mary's mediation is to be seen as co-extensive with the redemption in its twofold phase.

It remains to explain precisely what is its nature under the aspect of what is called, more or less appropriately, the distribution of graces. The very idea of distribution makes us think of a treasure which has been acquired: something inert, which is given out in the manner of a prize or a reward. It suggests that the grace is broken up into separate entities, isolated from uncreated grace, and it is difficult to understand why each, thus distributed, must without exception pass through Mary's hands. We must rise above such imagery, such "atomism," and grasp the truth that our Lady's mediation is simply her complete union with every aspect of the mystery of Christ, who is the one Mediator between God and men.

MEDIATION IN CHRIST

In order to understand this mediation positively, we must not think of it as something situated, as it were, beside, but *in* the one and only mediation of our Lord. She may be called a Mediatrix with the Mediator, but it would be more correct to say that she is such in and by the

Mediator. Properly speaking, her mediation is not between Christ and us, but in Christ between God and us. It can only be a cause for rejoicing to find a Lutheran theologian, Hans Asmussen, in accord upon this point with Catholic doctrine in his little book, *Maria, die Mutter Gottes*—"Mary the Mother of God"—where he sets out to speak not of a mediation of Mary "side by side with that of Christ," but of a "mediation *in* Christ." [1] This is an important step in the right direction taken by one of our separated brethren.

We must also distinguish the two very different occasions of Mary's mediation to which we have already drawn attention, at the Annunciation and on Calvary. At the former, Mary is really the representative of mankind, and utters her consent in the name of mankind. She does truly stand between God and man. On Calvary, however, it is Christ who represents humanity and offers sacrifice. It is his own mediation which includes that of his Mother, his own sacrifice which takes in hers. These two points of view must not be forgotten, for her mediation has, if we may thus express it, changed its direction in transit, remaining real while on a lower plane. Having made this remark, we would wish to answer the question which naturally arises: in carrying out her office of mediation, does Mary do so from God's side or from that of mankind?

MEDIATION IN CHRIST GLORIFIED

To reply by stating that Mary does so only from the latter, would be to exclude in fact every function properly called mediatory in which Mary transmits something to men on the part of God, and the Church cannot admit this unilateral point of view.

[1] *Evangelisches Verlagswerk,* Stuttgart, ed. 1951, p. 51.

It is true that Mary stands on the side of men, if by that we mean that she is purely a creature, created from nothing like every one of us, and that it is to the merits of Christ alone that she owes her exemption from original sin and her other privileges. No Catholic has ever held the senseless idea of adoring Mary, and to continue obstinately to accuse the Catholic Church of so doing is simply foolish. But the whole problem is to know whether the fact that every Christian is associated with our Lord does not involve him in the resurrection of Christ, and whether the whole Church Triumphant does not in Christ enter into participation of the effective royalty of its Head.

It suffices to read St Paul and understand how far in his eyes the Christian, "buried together with Christ," baptized into his death, is risen again with him and is a co-heir of his kingdom. Is not the very triumph of Christ to associate us with himself in his own triumph; is it not the glory of his one and only mediation that it should be communicated to his members, in the proportion of the closeness of the bond which binds them to him; is it not the fulfilling of his promise: "I have given them the privilege which thou gavest to me"? [2]

Is not this communion with Christ in his sanctifying power the supreme achievement, in its fullest intensity, of the communion of the elect in Christ glorified, the source of life? Did not our Lord promise such union to his Apostles in the triumphant words: "I promise you, in the new birth, when the Son of Man sits on the throne of his glory, you also shall sit there on twelve thrones, you who have followed me, and shall be judges over the twelve tribes of Israel"? [3] That promise enables us to catch a glimpse of the mystery of the triumphal communion with Christ, the Mediator of all graces. For it is indeed in life and in death

[2] John 17. 22.
[3] Matt. 19. 28.

that each of the elect is in Christ, and Mary more than any other.

If the saints are seated beside God in virtue of their incorporation with the glorious humanity of Christ, Mary, the Queen of Saints and their Mother, has a unique place in that royalty. The doctrine of her universal mediation becomes clearer if we understand that all the saints in heaven, according to their rank, and within their own limits, are also mediators with the one Mediator.

We say "within their own limits," for every saint shares in that mediation of Christ according to his personal and particular vocation, whereas Mary shares in that same mediation with incomparable fullness in the measure of her universal vocation of Mother of all living, in the measure of her function and the fullness of her adhesion to God. She is so united to Christ that no aspect of his mediation is unknown to her; she embraces all its extent, all its circumference. Seen thus, the Assumption of Mary is only the echo of the Ascension of her divine Son; and her universal mediation is but the pure triumph of the Mediator, the supreme success of his grace victorious in a creature.

Finally, we should notice that, unlike the saints, Mary has not merited this rôle of distributor of all graces subsequently to their acquisition. By her consent at the Annunciation, and her compassion on Calvary, she has shared in the name of us all in the saving act itself of the redemption. By way of her, all mankind has received salvation; in her every soul will henceforth be open to redeeming grace; her universal mediation of today prolongs her intervention of yesterday.

SUBORDINATED MEDIATION

Nevertheless, there is nothing arbitrary in her influence. Mary does not intervene in the distribution of graces as an autonomous sovereign, without any link of subordination to the power of Christ, but the harmony between the Mother and the Son is such that the sovereignty which Mary shares is but the faithful echo of that of Jesus; the agreement between them is so radical that their desires are identified. Mary does what she wishes, but with that freedom belonging to the true children of God, for whom to serve is to reign, and to will is to adhere to him. The mere hypotheses of an opposition, or clash of wills, is unthinkable, and we must banish ruthlessly all that popular imagery which would represent Mary as being more merciful to mankind than is her Son. When expounding a subject one is easily tempted to exaggerate it and isolate it from the context. Thus, when we speak of the redemption, and emphasize the love of the Son who is there delivering himself up to die, we must be careful not to lose sight of the love of the Father, who is and remains the source of all that love which glows in the heart of the Son. The divine drama of Calvary is not a struggle between Jesus and his Father, but a mystery in which two wills are fused into one and the same will that mankind should be saved.

Likewise, to depict Mary as the Mother of Mercy, pleading our cause with a Son who is our judge, would be to misrepresent that participation which is hers even in the mercy of that Son, who makes use of her the better to touch us. Michaelangelo's fresco of the Last Judgement in the Sistine Chapel in Rome, where Mary is shown holding back the avenging arm of the Judge, seems at first sight to be inspired by this false notion; but in fact, in the opinion of the best critics, it is a startling representation of the fundamental union between Mother and Son in the office of mediation. The whole fresco, inspired by the definitions of the Council of Trent, shows us Mary so close beside her Son as to share in the aureola of glory emanating from the glorified Christ. She does not at all turn aside his arm, but, according to authentic theological teaching, enters into his power.

On this point of doctrine there can be no ambiguity. Our Lady has not been given to us in order to be more approachable than God, but to show how very approachable God is in her. Instinctively we might be tempted to think of God as a stern judge, and thus, as it were, erect a screen between him and ourselves. Lest his love should be dimmed for us by the cloud of our fears, he has willed to show us that he does indeed love us, and that "with a mother's love." Mary helps us the better to realize how near he is, and any other explanation is an insult to him. When we stress one truth, we must never forget the truth which is complementary to it, and piety needs none of our extremes. Magnesium flashes may dazzle, but there is always the risk of their leaving in the shade the integral truth of the matter involved.

Moreover, we must never stop at a saint in himself or for his own sake, on pain of falsifying the dependence upon which rests his reality. Saints are beings who are splendidly relative and not absolutes. Each makes evident the love of God as an electric bulb does the current to which it is attached. The more closely he is united to God, the more luminous and radiant he becomes, but it is the power of Christ passing and working through him. It is not the saints who are wonderful, but God who is wonderful in his saints. God is the glory of Mary, as it is his love that shines forth in her. Such is the life-giving truth.

DIRECT MEDIATION

While Mary's mediation is subordinated to that of Christ, it is yet also direct mediation which is not that of an intermediary. She is not a kind of secondary mediator. Christ alone is the Mediator in the full sense of the word, and Mary does not contribute anything additional which is necessary to his mediation. Nor does he need any instrument to carry out his own redeeming mission. Nor is she an intermediary, interposing herself between him and us, for it is from his fullness that we receive grace, and that immediately and directly. There is no room for a second "capital" grace, and if Mary's part is often likened to that of the neck, or the heart, in the mystical Body, these similes are not to be pressed.

The Blessed Virgin is not an intermediary between Christ and us but a Mediatrix. The mediator does not interpose himself, does not isolate one from the other those whom he has the task to bring together. He does not set them at a distance from each other, but draws them together, brings each into the presence of the other. As wrote Mgr Kerkhofs of Liège: "The child who in order to kiss its father climbs on to a chair, or asks its mother to lift it up, does not thereby embrace him less directly, and does not raise the chair or the mother as an obstacle between its heart and the object of its filial love." [4] Just as the hand is not an intermediate object—as would be for example a stick—but the limb whereby I touch a person, so a saint and, *a fortiori,* Mary, is as the limb whereby I touch Christ. And she is eminently such; there is no danger of separation or wall of partition. Mary is not set between Christ and ourselves to keep us at a distance from him, but she is precisely the means chosen by God in order that there may be no distance between us, and that we may be sure of drawing near to him.

As a result of that fear of her being interposed between us and our Lord, we forget how truly, far from being a hindrance to our seeing him, Mary is completely "transparent" as it were. Far from being someone apart, every-

[4] "Marie Mediatrix de toutes les grâces" in *Rev. Eccl. de Liège,* t. 13, 1921–2, p. 91.

thing in our Lady is referred to her divine Son, or as says Cardinal Bérulle, she is "pure capacity" for possessing Jesus and helping us to do so. If he could declare: "Whoever has seen me has seen the Father," [5] she might say, by analogy and *mutatis mutandis*: "Whoever sees me sees my Son." In her is realized in a degree never hitherto attained, St Paul's words: "For me life means Christ." [6] Jesus, her Son, is her life, not only in the moral sense, as is the case for every earthly mother, but in the ontological sense also. It is not she who lives, but Christ who lives in her.

The saints have understood this better than anyone else, and St Louis Marie de Montfort has expressed it in unsurpassed language. "Let no one imagine," he writes, "that because she is a creature Mary is a hindrance to union with the Creator; it is no longer Mary who lives, but only Jesus Christ, only God, who lives in her. She is transformed in God in a degree higher than that of St Paul and the other saints than heaven is higher than earth. Mary was made for God alone, and far is she from causing a soul to stop at herself. On the contrary, she casts it upon God, and unites it to him the more perfectly according as the soul is more united to her. She is the wonderful echo of God, and when a soul calls 'Mary,' she answers only 'God.' When, with Elizabeth, we call her Blessed, she only glorifies God." Always and everywhere, she simply leads us to Jesus, as a river leads us to the sea. In the words of Claudel, she is "the Catholic highroad whereby we travel to God," on the understanding, however, that we do not merely pass through her, as by a passage-way in order to find Christ, for he lives in her and gives himself to us through her.

[5] John 14. 9.
[6] Phill. 1. 21.

MARY'S MEDIATION IN THE TEACHING OF THE CHURCH

Therefore the Church teaches the doctrine of Mary's mediation in the present. Is this a dogma of faith? No, but it is a truth of faith admitted and recognized by the ordinary *magisterium* of the Church, and as such is proposed to us.

There is a tendency at the present day to allege that a doctrine is neither certain nor revealed until it has been solemnly defined either by the pope speaking *ex cathedra* or by a General Council in union with him. We must not think that only truths thus defined are proposed to us as absolutely certain. Such an attitude was expressly condemned in the *Syllabus,* which rejects the proposition that "the strict obligation which binds Catholic teachers and writers is limited to the statements proposed to the faithful, to be believed by all, as dogmas of faith by an infallible decision of the Church." Furthermore, the Vatican Council explicitly recognizes a twofold teaching of the Church, that which is given by way of solemn definition and that imparted by way of her ordinary *magisterium:* that is, the teaching which she gives to her children by her normal, daily instruction. This latter teaching can be gathered from the documents addressed by the Holy See to the universal Church, from the pastoral letters of the bishops, from the catechisms which are the expression of the common instruction of the Church, and also from the prayers of the liturgy in universal use, according to the saying, *Lex orandi est lex credendi:* as is the prayer, so is the belief.

In his Encyclical *Humani Generis,* Pius XII reminded us that the authentic interpretation of the revealed deposit of faith is entrusted to the *magisterium* alone, "which car-

ries out this duty, as has often happened in the course of
the centuries, either by the ordinary or extraordinary exercise of that power."

If we bear these principles in mind, we must conclude
that the mediation of our Lady comes within the *magisterium* and therefore requires our acceptance. It is not
requisite that it should be defined as a dogma binding
upon all Catholics, and it belongs to the Church alone to
judge as to the opportuneness of a definition which hitherto she has not considered necessary.

OTHER ASPECTS OF THE DOCTRINE

The mediation of Mary in its present phase, which is
heavenly, is not contested between theologians, who consider only the *mode*—the manner—of this intervention.
In its earthly phase, which has passed away, her mediation, which is identified with the Co-redemption, is under
discussion, but this is less the case than formerly. The
declarations of the *magisterium* clearly favour the recognition of that immediate collaboration at the cross. Let us
add that as for the mediation in the present, which is identified with the distribution of graces, everyone is in agreement in emphasizing the place of the intercession, the
"all-powerful supplication of Mary." This mediation is
brought into play even if the one who prays is not con-
sciously invoking her, or even when such a one is invoking some other saint.

Benedict XV made an important statement with respect
to this matter at the reading of the decree approving the
two miracles presented for the canonization of St Joan of
Arc. One of these took place at Lourdes, and the Pro-
motor of the Faith—the "devil's advocate"—objected
that the evidence for the miracle was inconclusive, since
it ought to be attributed to our Lady and not to Blessed

Joan. The pope's answer to that difficulty enables us to see rather how universal is Mary's part. If, he said, when considering prodigies it was fitting to recognize Mary's intervention, through whom, according to the divine will, every grace and every benefit comes to us: it was impossible to deny that in one of the alleged miracles that mediation of the Blessed Virgin had been made manifest in an altogether special manner: "We think that God so disposed matters in order to remind the faithful that they must never exclude the remembrance of Mary, even when it seems that a miracle should be attributed to the intercession or mediation of a saint or a Beatus." Here we see the Church, by the voice of Benedict XV, associating Mary with our Lord in the universal dispensing of all graces.

Nor can we fail to be impressed by the part attributed to her in their conversion by so many converts. Not only in the ages of faith, but even in our rationalistic times, we can find very many such attestations. It is enough to mention such as Newman, Alphonse Ratisbonne and Huysmans, among so many who have borne similar witness to this fact.

We have said that theologians are divided as to the manner in which this office of Mediatrix is to be understood. Some equate it with the moral causality proper to intercession and leave it at that. To others, it goes beyond that of pure prayer and involves a more direct influence, although such is always derived from and subordinated to the unique mediation of Christ.

In his *Essai de Synthèse Mariale,* Fr Nicolas, O.P., indicates his preference for that more direct intervention:

It is impossible to deny to Mary what can belong to other creatures, namely the power to enlighten our souls, and that very often: to bring about in them many a movement by direct influence, to make them aware of an impression like a presence. Such is borne out by the experience of many saints. Why should we not be inclined to attribute to the direct intervention of her soul in our souls all that is of the nature of a preparation, disposing the soul for grace? There would thus be a wonderful correspondence between her mother's part, which consists above all in offering the matter for the Incarnation, and her part as Mediatrix, which would consist in preparing the human matter for the descent of grace at the same time as she calls down that grace through her prayer.[7]

For our own part, we gladly make our own the carefully expressed and wise words of Abbé Laurentin, who is of the same opinion as Fr Nicolas. After showing the place for the effective intercession of Mary, he asks: "What is the manner of this effective action?" He answers thus, and with his words we shall conclude.

Without entering into the discussions which arise out of this question, we may propose some precise statements. The love of Mary for her children is, as we have seen, full of desires and intentions which reflect, in the heart of this woman overwhelmed with grace, the will of God himself. She repeats to God what together with him she wishes, rather as a wife likes to talk with her husband, and he to hear from her some cherished thought, some secret wish. How far do these desires reach to men? Through their own power they reach men in intention, that is, in thought, but not really, that is, in action. For human wishes, however earnest they may be, do not carry in themselves the principle of their realization. Only God can fulfil Mary's supernatural desires for her children. Must we, then, think of an action taking place in two stages? As we see in the Bible, Bethsabee when she entrusts her request to David, then leaves him to act.[8] On this hypothesis, Mary would pray and then stand by as a spectator while the divine power manifests itself. This material and earthly misrepresentation would fail to recognize the spiritual and heavenly communion implied by the beatific vision. We must distrust the imagination. As we

[7] See *Marie*, t. I, p. 739. Beauchesne, Paris.
[8] 3 Kings 1.

refused to disassociate Mary's intentions from those of God, let us be careful not to disassociate God's action and hers. Heaven is in fact, for Mary as for all the elect, but in a higher degree, a life with everything in common: a total interior communion with God. Hence we must not imagine that between her and God there takes place a dialogue with successive answers, as in a game when a ball is sent and returned by two players. As the divine intention inspires and penetrates the interior intercession of Mary, so is the power of God likewise interior to her. The divine power supplies for that powerlessness and sterility which mark all human wishes. By that interior and delicate fusion, Mary's desires attain their object, not only intentionally but really: for that same power inspires and penetrates her prayer, and gives to her desires which, like all desires, are inchoate and "sketchy," the power to attain their objects.

We cannot further precisely explain the manner of this interpenetration, which is obviously vastly different from that which exists in the case of the sacraments, but seemingly it is fitting that a mother should thus reach her children, not only in intention but really, and that it is difficult to explain otherwise the experience, so striking and so frequent, of the "presence of Mary" in the souls of the saints.[9]

[9] *Court Traité de Théologie Mariale*, pp. 100-1, Paris, Lethiel-Leux, 1953.

CHAPTER X

THE PRACTICAL ASPECT
OF MARY'S MEDIATION

UNION WITH CHRIST IN MARY

If our Lady's mediation is such as we have just explained, it is normal that this teaching should be translated into action in every Christian life. This concrete and daily adhesion to God's plan can be called union lived in Mary, or better, union with Christ in Mary, but it must always be understood that the term of the union is Christ and the Blessed Trinity. Our human ideas are poor and defective when it comes to expressing the inexpressible, and our vocabulary causes us to use the word "union" with respect to Mary as well as our Lord, while in reality the significance of the term is obviously quite different in each case. In order to express the mystery of the divine action in Mary and through Mary, language needs very careful handling. Let us first say what this union is not, so as to prevent all misunderstanding.

At no price can there be any question of an indwelling of Mary in the human soul: that is reserved to the Trinity and to Christ, according to St Paul's words: "I am alive or rather, not I; it is Christ that lives in me." [1] Moreover,

[1] Gal. 2. 20.

as we know, it is not the sacred humanity that dwells in us; that humanity is present only in heaven and in the Blessed Sacrament. It is by reason of his Godhead—for he is a divine Person—that we have the right to say that our Lord abides in the soul of each one of us. Still less can we speak of Mary's so doing. Her vocation is to give us Christ; her part is not to dwell herself in us but to make Christ live in our souls. By her whole being, she is the one who conceives and bears our Lord, who identifies us not with herself but with him; who forms in us the image of Christ. Better than St Paul, she can say, "My little children, I am in travail over you . . . until I can see Christ's image formed in you!" [2]

She forms Christ in us by assimilating us to him, and thus allows us to be integrated with him. Mary, who does not exist for herself, works only for her Son. Moreover, as we have said, Christ alone is the source of grace in its fullness of which we receive the overflow. Yet this overflowing of "capital" grace does not take place without Mary; our Lord plays therein the part of Head and Mary that of mother; the grace itself is not divided and belongs wholly and entirely to Christ.

As there is no question of any indwelling of Mary, so also her mediation has nothing in common with any kind of "substitution," as though she caused our personality to disappear and takes its place in our relations with God or with our neighbour. To live in Mary does not mean at all such a strange "alchemy," and we must be careful not to attribute such an imaginary aberration to spiritual writers who extol the union with Christ in Mary.

If, for example, they exhort us to advance towards God by offering him the faith and love of our Lady, and by disappearing before her, or in her presence, there is no question whatever of substituting her for ourselves, as

[2] Gal. 4. 2.

though appealing to her mediation suppressed all active collaboration on our part. When the liturgy puts upon our lips before Holy Communion those great words, "Lord, look not upon my sins, but upon the faith of thy Church," that does not mean that we are dispensed from believing on our own account, but that there is given to our weak, personal faith an amplitude, an exaltation, a catholicity which is beyond our own capacity. It is the same if we ask God to look not upon our faith but upon that of Mary who is, moreover, the Mother of that Church which the liturgy is calling to our aid. When writers speak of Mary as "supplying for us," they mean nothing more than this. It is enough to read, for instance, the prayer: *O Maria, Virgo et Mater:* "O Mary, Virgin and Mother, behold I have received thy beloved Son . . ." which is to be found in the Missal among the prayers suggested as thanksgiving after Mass, to see how the Church asks our Lady to give thanks in our place without fear of falling into some sort of Quietism: "I humbly and lovingly offer him to you, that you may clasp him in your arms, love him with your heart, and offer him in supreme homage to the Holy Trinity." The most authentic writings upon Mary are full of similar prayers.

NATURE OF OUR DEPENDENCE UPON MARY

Now in order to explain practically the nature of this dependence upon the Mother of God, which is inherent in the divine plan, we must consider for a moment the different ways in which a child is dependent upon its mother. It suffices to compare their ages to see that a youth of twenty is not dependent upon her as is a child of ten, still less an infant of a year or a day. The dependence is greatest in the case of the unborn child, and therefore, however defective and relative the simile may be, it is the one spiritual writers suggest to us as typifying the state of dependence to be attained in order that the Christ-life may grow in us. When Nicodemus heard our Lord speak of a new birth necessary for those who would enter the kingdom of heaven, he exclaimed: "Why, how is it possible that a man should be born when he is already old? Can he enter a second time into his mother's womb, and so come to birth?" [3] We know our Lord's answer: and there are still disciples of Nicodemus who find it difficult to understand the way of spiritual childhood upon which we must enter if we would live both as children of God and children of Mary; since Christ himself lived this double and yet single life. Let us consider more closely some aspects of our dependence upon Mary.

The simile just suggested has the advantage of making us grasp at once the nature of the total dependence of the child, such as each one of us is. The unborn child is enveloped on every side, nothing of it escapes from the milieu in which it exists. It feels and breathes through its mother, is carried about and moved by her only. The doctrine of Mary's mediation possesses this character of totality. She is universal Mediatrix, every grace comes to us by means of her, in the strict sense of the words. We are still far from having understood what this involves, and our religious instruction should enter into greater detail concerning the rich significance of this influence, scrutinize its many aspects and analyse this sort of "omnipresence."

"Everything is grace," says Bernanos, and that is true, but if everything is grace, everything is *ipso facto* under our Lady's influence, and that influence extends very far. It is not enough to state that her mediation is universal; priests and teachers must show in detail how such mediation is effectively realized in the Christian's every gesture,

[3] John 3. 4.

and how she marks everything with her influence of grace, from the sign of the cross which we make and which she taught to Bernadette, to the fruitful reception of the sacraments, not excluding all the various activities, sacred and secular, to which she is no stranger.

In the case of the young child's relations with its mother, this dependence is a condition of life, and on the supernatural plane the case is similar as regards the birth and development of the Christ-life within us. Everything depends upon Mary; there is no question of asking ourselves to what share of our devotion she has a right. We must give it all to our Lord: "You belong to Christ"—but we must give all to him through and by Mary.

CONSCIOUS AND UNCONSCIOUS DEPENDENCE

The unborn child is unaware of the dependence that gives it life unknown to itself, and likewise the distribution of graces in our favour takes place whether we know it or not, since it is inherent in the very working of grace. In order that she should intervene in the granting of a prayer, it is not necessary to invoke Mary explicitly. The words of Benedict XV, already quoted, formally remind us of that; though this is not to say that for us to be aware of such intervention is not of importance for the development of our Catholic life, as is also our willing and active cooperation. It is in the divine order that a baptized Christian should understand and ratify as an adult this spiritual motherhood, so that it may attain its full development in him. Hence the importance of an enlightened and solid devotion to our Lady.

Throughout the Christian centuries Mary has been forming saints, but there was a time when the doctrine of her universal mediation had not yet been clearly seen, and her part in developing Christian life was somewhat obscured. It is remarkable when we notice how many of the saints canonized in the last hundred years have been strongly influenced by their conscious union with Mary. Once the doctrine became explicit, they lived it with a rare intensity, which imparts to their holiness a certain striking "Marian" radiance, while their unanimity on this matter is very significant. The same may be said concerning some of the apostles of modern times. We are obliged to acknowledge that the men whose apostolic action has been particularly fruitful have made a conspicuous place in their spiritual lives for Mary. To mention only contemporaries, we may think of Cardinal Mercier, Abbé Godin, Brother Mutien Marie, Edel Quinn, and many another.[4] There, again, we have the truth confirmed by experience.

PERMANENT AND WILLING DEPENDENCE

As a child grows older, it becomes progressively less dependent upon its mother, and enjoys a life of its own. It becomes increasingly autonomous with the years, but such is not our case in regard to Mary's motherhood. When we grow in grace, that does not mean that she effaces herself and that her relation to us becomes less close. On the contrary, her growing influence increases the Christ-life in us, just as a higher voltage increases the light and warmth of the electric light or heater. Mary is not eclipsed in the soul that is becoming more Christlike; her action cannot be separated from that of her Son, for it is a modality of the latter, and is increased in proportion as he attains to his full stature in us. It is vitally important that we should understand this law of life, for otherwise we should regard Mary's part as simply a passing phase, and her intervention as something belonging to a pre-

[4] To these may surely be added Pius XII. (Tr.)

liminary stage instead of remaining a constant factor in the developing of our spiritual life. At the end of a life which has been faithful to grace, the saint is more than ever his Mother's child. Such is the triumph of the Master's promise: "Unless you become as little children, you shall not enter the kingdom of heaven."

That renewal of spiritual youth and childlike joy is a test of genuine Christlike holiness. We are not advancing towards death but towards life. Supernaturally, we pass not from life to death, but from life to life, and from life eternal, lived here already on earth in the dimness of faith, to life eternal in the full brightness of the beatific vision. It is normal that devotion towards Mary should be marked with this sign of spiritual youth and this seal of joy.

And this lifelong dependence rests upon a simple act of will on our part, as simple as that whereby I decide to switch on a light. My hand goes to the switch, but it is not the switch but the lamp that gives brightness and warmth. The case is similar here. I pause a moment to unite myself to Mary's action in my soul, and forthwith it is the life of Christ which intensifies my soul's life and action. But the contact has fulfilled its purpose. As the soul goes forward in the spiritual life, these contacts—a moment of recollection, an ejaculatory prayer, an interior glance—are multiplied and finally coalesce, so that this life in Mary becomes continuous; and this is the term of all piety towards our Lady which is worthy of the name.

It is that progression in love experienced in happy families. As the years go by, love has less need of being shown by outward behaviour; rather, it increases in depth, and welds souls together almost without their knowing it. But to reach this state of union we must begin by multiplying our gestures and deliberate acts. Progressively, these repeated acts of conscious union with Mary will bring about a *state* of union, when there will no longer be any need of this multiplicity of conscious acts, and which will continue to simplify and develop unto eternal life.

PURIFICATION AND UNIFICATION

This initial act of conscious union with our Lady has the immediate effect of preparing us for the action of grace. Always and everywhere, Mary is "Our Lady of Advent": she who predisposes us, opens our hearts, strengthens our weakness and overcomes our resistance. It is her special function to free us from all that is opposed to God's action in us. She detaches us from ourselves, purifies us, and unburdens us so as to prepare ample room in us for our Lord. For such, in fine, is her whole office. I unite myself to her, and to her influence, now in order that Christ may grow in me.

It is because union with Mary is essentially at the base of sacrifice, of determined renunciation of self, of interior detachment, that it is a school of humility and, therefore, of holiness, for the two terms are correlative. God can fill us only if we are emptied of self, and the perfect accord which we find in the testimony of the saints concerning this effect of dependence upon Mary in our lives is impressive.

"We make more progress," writes one of them, "in a short time by submission to and dependence upon Mary, than during whole years of self-will and dependence upon ourselves. . . . We advance to our Lord by giant strides by the same road which he took in order to come to us. . . . True devotion to the Blessed Virgin is a short cut which soon leads us to Jesus. . . . It is in Mary's womb that children become patriarchs in understanding, holiness, experience and wisdom, and attain in a few years to the fullness of age in him." [5]

[5] *True Devotion to Mary*, nos. 155–6.

St Pius X has echoed this teaching in his Encyclical *Ad Diem illum*. "There is no way more sure and speedy whereby man may be united to Jesus Christ than Mary and to obtain by means of Jesus Christ that perfect adoption of children which renders us holy and without spot before God. . . . No one in the world knew Jesus as she did, and there is no better teacher and guide to make him known to mankind. . . . Hence it follows . . . that, likewise, no one can unite men to him as she can" (February 1904).

But all this is still only the negative aspect of Mary's activity. Positively, this initial act of union lends itself to a great variety of religious attitudes and sanctifies us in many different ways. There are many ways of praying and acting "in Mary." An example drawn from the daily recitation of the Psalms will make this clearer. The Church teaches us that we may say them in several ways. The individual may pray them in his own name, as also in the name of the Church, in the name of Mary, in the name of our Lord, or in union with the Holy Spirit who has inspired them. Each of these different manners of reciting them will differ according to the method adopted, although ontologically each of these aspects includes the others. To pray "in Mary," that is to say in union of soul with her, will take on also diverse forms. Sometimes a mother helps her child to pray alone, at another time she prays with it, guiding it, whispering the words, leading it on. Again, she may pray alone, and the child joins in her prayer and repeats the words with her. It is always the same motherly training at work, but according to differences of outlook, and the same is true as regards the different attitudes we may take towards our Lady.

The following quotations provide an example of one way of "praying in Mary." Instead of offering God its own personal thanksgiving, a soul may unite itself to Mary in order to offer him the actual gratitude of Mary: "I feel in my soul the thanksgiving of Mary. I am continually thanking the Blessed Trinity for what has been done to her and for her: the Father for having created her for his Son, the Son for having accepted her for his Mother, the Holy Spirit for having taken her for his bride. . . .When I say: 'In the name of the Father, and of the Son and of the Holy Ghost,' I must say it attentively and reverently. It is Mary who is greeting the Holy Spirit through me." [6]

Here are some other quotations of the same kind: "I am terribly lukewarm at present, but I am helping myself to recover by offering to the Blessed Trinity the pure and inexpressible love of my heavenly Mother. She is everything to me, and everything she has is mine. That is why I am not troubled by my spiritual wretchedness, my sins and my lukewarmness."

"United to Mary, life will be for us a perpetual *Deo gratias* and *Domine, non sum dignus.* There is a world of meaning in a simple, calm and intense 'Thank you!' Therefore, here on earth I long to be the 'Thank you' of the Blessed Virgin. It seems to me as though she must be pleased with my poor attempts to thank the Father, the Son and the Holy Spirit for all they have done in her and by her means."

What we have just said about "prayer in Mary" holds good, *mutatis mutandis,* for "action in Mary." There is a way of thinking, speaking, acting and living in Mary that translates into deeds that moral identification, and puts into practice that spiritual motherhood in the detail of apostolic life, or in works of charity. Someone has said that "to speak to souls in Mary is to see in each of the hearers not just an inquirer but a child, and to be convinced that it is not my human eloquence but my degree of mother-love for each of them that will be the instrument of grace to touch them. It is still the same principle,

[6] Quoted in *La Vie d'Union à Marie,* Neubert. (Paris, *Alsatia,* 1954, p. 303.)

the same secret: activity is fruitful when Mary detaches us from ourselves so as to prepare the way for God. A soul must be Mary, if Jesus is to be at his ease in it and able to work through it. He is so happy to come and dwell in a soul that is established in her, and he makes use of it forthwith, in order to radiate himself in one who thus offers himself as an instrument.

To conclude this analysis, we may say that this life in Mary tends to become increasingly simple. Living thus dependent upon her is rather like driving a car. At first, the driver concentrates his attention, perhaps rather anxiously, upon the car and his driving, and sees little of the landscape. As he becomes more experienced, however, while still aware that he is in the car, he looks about him constantly and sees the surrounding view. Such is the story of the moral development of devotion to Mary in a soul. It exemplifies to the letter those words of Saint-Exupéry: "To love is not to look at each other, but to look in the same direction."

That such is truly the case is verified daily by experience. "Gradually," wrote a soul devoted to our Lady, "a change is taking place in my relations with the Blessed Virgin. No longer is she 'there beside me,' and I 'here.' Instead of loving her as apart, with all my strength, praying to her, offering her beauty and perfection to the Holy Trinity, I feel as though I were somehow identified with her. She seems to be in me and I in her; it is as though we were identified in one single being, and completely turned towards our Lord, towards the Holy Spirit, towards the Holy Trinity. Since I felt like this, I rarely think explicitly of Mary, but I am very much aware of being with her, directed towards God with her, and also to all that is of God in heaven and on earth."

Such is truly the normal triumph of life lived in Maria Mediatrix.

MYSTICAL UNION

Beyond the ordinary acquired union of which we have just been speaking, which is within the reach of all, there exists a union with Mary which can properly be called mystical, and here there opens up before us a wide field for thought and study which has as yet been little explored. A theologian, Père Neubert, who has specialized in Marian theology, has treated of it with both learning and competence in his *Vie d'Union à Marie*. He writes:

> The essence of ordinary mystical union with Mary seems to consist in an interior awareness of an action, attributed to her, which perfects the dispositions of the soul by adding to them the dispositions of Mary, and directs that soul's activity according to the intentions of the Mother, in view of a closer union with God. The soul may be more or less intensely conscious of this action, the strength and all-pervading nature of which may become such that it feels as though it were possessed by Mary.
>
> It is a matter of an interior presence of a special character. Such a privileged soul is aware that it loves our Lord with the heart of Mary, and Mary with his heart. In this mystical experience, Mary seems somehow to take possession of the soul's activities, so that it comes to think, act and love consciously by her and in her, and she seems to act upon it almost continuously.

When somebody asked the Venerable Louis Cestac if he saw our Blessed Lady, he replied: "No, I do not see her, but I am aware of her as the horse is aware of the hand of the rider who guides it." People who are in this state express themselves in various ways, but all tend in the same direction. One theologian speaks of the "virtual" presence of Mary, in order to emphasize that there is no question here of an indwelling of Mary, or an identification with her, but of a presence of influence and action.

Only a few explicit testimonies to this experience are to

be found before the seventeenth century, but the fact of this mystical union is attested by too many trustworthy witnesses to be rejected. We might mention a whole line of such privileged souls: St John Eudes, St Louis Marie Grignon de Montfort, M. Olier, Fr Louis Cestac, Fr Chaminade, Mother Mary of the Incarnation, Fr Jacquier. We can find a trace of it in the life of Sister Colette du Saint Sacrement, a Poor Clare of Besançon (1905), and in that of Lucie Christine, published by Père Poulain, S.J.[7] In the spiritual diary of the latter are to be found these characteristic lines: "The particular quality of this union is that the soul feels that the Blessed Virgin is as a bond of love between God and itself, as a divine means of reaching him." It cannot be denied that similar traces are to be found also in the autobiography of St Teresa of Lisieux, who refers to this presence of Mary in the early years of her life at Carmel. "There seemed to be a veil thrown over all earthly things, so far as I was concerned . . . I felt as though I were entirely hidden beneath our Lady's veil. Just then I was refectorian, and I remember how I carried out my duties as though it were not I who was doing them; it was as though someone had lent me a body. I remained like that during a whole week. It was a supernatural state difficult to explain. Only God can put us into it, and sometimes it is enough to detach a soul from

[7] To these might be added an example in the case of Dom Pie de Hemptinne, a young monk of the Abbey of Maredsous, in Belgium, and a spiritual son of Abbot Marmion. It is taken from a private letter.

"I had made up my mind not to write this, but to wait for an opportunity to tell you . . . but I can no longer hide from you an important favour which our Lord has shown me, scarcely a month ago. He has united my heart to that of Mary, our Mother. I am now able to live with her as with Jesus, without the help of a rosary, or anything else except love. I find it impossible to think of him without thinking of her. I unite myself to him in order to love Mary, and I take refuge in her heart in order to abandon myself to him. . . . I cannot write of all the effects this has had upon me. See *Une âme bénédictine*, Paris, 1926. (*Trans.*)

earth for ever" (*Novissima Verba,* July 11th). Evidently she has here weighed her words, and the occurrence was a landmark in her life.

The most explicit and lasting experience of this kind is beyond doubt that of the Flemish recluse, Marie de Sainte Thérèse (Marie Petyt), a Carmelite Tertiary, who lived at Malines in the seventeenth century and was made known by her spiritual director, the Carmelite Fr Michel de Saint Augustin. He published some valuable notes on "this gift of the presence of Mary, lived and felt," as she explained it. The recluse was aware of Mary not as dwelling in her but as acting in her by means of an influence of grace in which she was aware of our Lady's personal touch. Born in 1623, Marie died in 1677, and so never knew the writings of St Louis Grignon de Montfort, who was born in 1673. This fact is worthy of notice as emphasizing the originality of the Tertiary's evidence. She herself thus describes this presence:

There are times when a spiritual life in Mary is shown to and given to me: a rest in Mary, a joy, a fusion, a loss (*sic*), a union in Mary. This is how it takes place: In all simplicity, completely detached and tranquil, when the mind is directed to God, and clinging to him in himself, without any imagery, in contemplation and fruition of that being who is absolutely simple, it happens that at the same time my soul is aware also of an adhesion to, a contemplation and a fruition of Mary, inasmuch as she is with God and united to him. Savouring God, I also savour Mary as though she were one with God. [She takes account of the reserve of certain spiritual authorities of her day:] This life in Mary does not please the majority of mystical and contemplative persons. To them it seems as though this life in Mary must be a hindrance to the purest union with God, to silent interior prayer, and so forth. As they understand the matter and imagine it, it seems to them too crude, too material, too complicated, because they do not grasp the real and simple way of practising it completely in the spirit.

Yet, after all, it is wholly the spirit which is working and guiding here, even if the sensitive powers seem to mingle a little activity with this contemplation, this attraction, this love on the part of the soul. In this case, there is not the slightest hindrance, or intermediary imposed between the supreme Good, the pure Being of God and the soul. Rather is the latter helped and enabled to reach God more easily, and be more perfectly established in him. [And she endeavours to explain further:] I do not really know whether I understand myself aright, but by means of this habit of thus possessing that lovable Mother in my heart and will, my spirit seems to be guided by, to live, so to speak, possessed by the spirit of Mary, equally in times of action and of suffering; it is as though the spirit of Mary does everything in me. . . . When we receive the grace of being able to contemplate God and love him in Mary, and by her being united to him, then God shows himself in Mary and by her as in a mirror.

We catch the echo of this spirituality in the words of a Flemish priest who died in 1926, and whose cause of beatification has been begun, Abbé Édouard Poppe: "To long after Mary," he wrote, "means that with our understanding we long to be of one mind with her, that our will may receive her strength, our entire being her spirit." And elsewhere, speaking of her part as our Mother, he adds: "She maintains us in the spiritual atmosphere of grace: a bright cloud, wherein we can abide and take shelter."

Still closer to us, the gift of a conscious presence of Mary is, beyond doubt, the key to the heroism of Edel Quinn, who died in the odour of sanctity in Nairobi in 1944, the examination of whose possible Cause has also begun, and whose life is a source of inspiration to many lay apostles throughout the world.

THE LESSON OF THE MYSTICS

This experience of our Lady's presence in the souls of the saints is a call to all of us to live better, in faith, the mystery of her mediation. Our union with Christ in Mary —whether acquired or by infusion it will sometimes be difficult to decide—ought to be integrated in our spiritual life, so that God can freely bestow his grace to the utmost. The mystics open up prospects before us. "Their existence," as Bergson said, "is an appeal." How can we close this chapter better than by recalling the grand passage from Fr Léonce de Grandmaison on their part in the Church, and applying it here to the line of Marian mystics whom we have mentioned?

The experiences of those forerunners, the forlorn hopes of our race, who set out in pursuit of the Unveiled Good, remain to us, consigned by them as the documents brought back by explorers of almost inaccessible lands. If we want to follow those bold travellers, and check their reports, it depends upon ourselves whether we accompany them in thought, and we can profit more in the schools of a Scott, a Roald Amundsen, a Sven Hedin, or an Ollone, than in that of a thousand stay-at-homes by whom we are surrounded. The great mystics are the pioneers and heroes of the fairest, the most desirable and the most marvellous of worlds. In their place and in their rank, they remain witnesses. After the great witness who revealed the Father to us: after the apostles and the martyrs, observing all due proportion and difference, the great mystics can say with the beloved disciple: "Our message concerns what we have heard about him, what our own eyes have seen of him." [8] And when we hear their account, our souls tremble with hope and expectation. They bear testimony to the loving presence of God in man. We owe to them that consolation of knowing and realizing that others have loved him, who deserves to be perfectly loved, better than we have done. They give us what is perhaps the fairest and sweetest of joys, as well as the most fruitful, because it is always a stimulus and an incentive—the joy of wondering admiration!

[8] 1 John 1. 1.

CHAPTER XI

MARY AND OUR TIMES

MARY AND THE APOSTOLIC RENEWAL

In ecclesiastical as in secular history, there are surface events and also strong undercurrents which control actual happenings. "Events," as Paul Valéry writes, "are only as the surface foam; what interests me is the sea." Our century is characterized by several currents of grace which, like the deep waves, uplift the whole Church. That is the Holy Spirit at work in souls. Two currents of devotion to Mary and of the apostolate are dominating the life of the Church today. We are living in an age of Mary. The proofs are so striking that there is no need to insist upon them. Popular movements testify to this fact. We have only to think of the crowds at Lourdes, Fatima, Czestochowa, Our Lady of Guadalupe, and so many other sanctuaries throughout the Christian world. Chosen groups of souls witness to it. Is it generally known that since the beginning of the nineteenth century more religious societies in honour of Mary have been founded than in all preceding ages of the Church? And what of the labour expended by theologians in scrutinizing ever more closely the mysteries connected with our Lady, such as the co-redemption, and the mediation, or relationship between her and the Church? Bishops the world over have witnessed to this since the consecration of the world to Mary in 1942 up to the Jubilee Year of Lourdes in 1958.

Such are some examples, chosen among many others, of the vast movement that is uplifting the Church and bearing it on to Mary in a soaring flight. Some years ago, when speaking of the contemporary generation, Fr Doncœur said: "Nourished upon sound doctrine, and the Eucharist, this generation will do much; but it has yet to discover the Blessed Virgin." That discovery is taking place before our eyes.

Side by side with this awakening, is taking place another. Acted upon by the same Spirit, our generation is finding again that apostolic sense, inherent in baptism, and confirmation, which is the crown of the earlier sacrament. Clergy and laity are becoming more vividly aware of their apostolic duty towards their brethren, and of its urgency.

Has the Holy Spirit, which is bringing about these movements, forged any link between them? Has his action followed paths which are simply parallel or even distinct? Must we not rather conclude that these graces concerning Mary and the apostolate are together following mysteriously along a road towards a point where they will meet, and that the time has come to accept or unite what in the sight of God belongs to the same divine will for the salvation of mankind: devotion to Mary and the duty of apostolic action?

This bond and spirit of union impose themselves upon us. The meeting of the two movements is not accidental, but brought about and willed as such by the Holy Spirit. Moreover, it belongs to the very logic of our faith. Since Pentecost, our Lady has been called to cooperate with that Spirit in the mission of the Church, and she is still carrying on her task. The alliance then made will never more be unmade; for her also, the promise made by God to his people holds good, that people of whom she is to be the fairest flower:

"Everlasting I will betroth thee to myself, favour and

redress and mercy of mine thy dowry; by the keeping of his troth thou shalt learn to know the Lord." [1] Spiritual Mother of the Church, that is the Mystical Body of Christ, Mary has only one desire: to cooperate in the invisible birth, in the development of the life of Christ in her children.

MOTHERHOOD OF MARY AND THE APOSTOLATE

This personal mission cannot normally be carried out by Mary without our cooperation. What she alone once did for her Son, she wills to continue through us in favour of his Mystical Body. Nazareth has become a wide world, but her mother's heart is not changed. It is not we who call upon her to help us in "our" apostolic labours, but she who invites us to share her mother's mission and continue her work.

In the first place, what she expects from us is not the tribute of our admiration but that of our cooperation. She wants us to make her intentions our own, so as the better to love her Son in our neighbour. She asks us to serve him in the person of another with infinite respect, seeing always, as she does, Jesus in every fellow creature, and approaching the latter not as though we are his superior nor even his equal, but as the inferior approaches his master. She wishes us to love that neighbour with the delicacy, tact and perseverance proper to a mother, who never forsakes her child even if it has wandered from the right path. She wants us to share her preferences, and enter lovingly into her ministry of mercy, among the strayed sheep of human society. In short, she wants us to show our love for her in a practical manner, by prolonging by our

[1] Osee 1. 10.

apostolic action her own spiritual motherhood which is ever at work.

So this "Marian" aspect of the apostolate is not accidental and optional; it is not a matter of our free choice and preference; and any apostolate which fails to take account of our Lady is lacking in something. Nor are we concerned with a personal monopoly, a distinctive note, or an original point of view, but simply with the normal practice of the Christian religion.

Let us make no mistake. If our apostolate is to be informed with the spirit of Mary, a few pious gestures before or after some activity, or a passing reference to her is not sufficient. No doubt, the love of children for their parents is sometimes expressed by a bouquet of flowers, but if it is sincere it must lie at the very centre of their everyday life. To honour our Lady intermittently, during the month of May or on some feast, is good, but it is far from sufficient. Devotion to her must be really rooted in her abiding motherhood; it is our apostolic activity itself which must be conceived and lived out as a prolongation of hers. It means a living union, a mediation fully practised. How otherwise could we love our Mother rightly than by entering into the mystery which lies at the very foundation of her vocation and her life? That is the mystery of her motherhood. It is not for us to pick and choose those of her prerogatives or virtues which we intend to honour or reproduce; we must enter into the mystery of Mary, such as God has willed it, and accept it in its fullness.

DEVOTION TO MARY IN ACTION AND LIFE

We have been too prone to conceive of devotion to our Lady as in the category of pious practices apart from action and life. That strong sense of the word "devotion," which has become weakened and sentimentalized, must be restored. The word has an active sense. It is derived from *de* and *vovere,* which means to devote oneself, hand oneself over completely, and implies essentially complete self-giving. When, in the Canon of the Mass, the celebrant commends to God the faithful "whose faith and devotion are known to thee," the word is used entirely in the sense given above, of active service.

No one has emphasized more strongly the vital link between devotion to the Mother of God and apostolic action than Frank Duff, the founder of the Legion of Mary, that worldwide movement so visibly marked with the signs of the supernatural. Its action is but the living commentary of these lines which sum up his thought:

> A real devotion to Mary attains its full development only in union with her. Of necessity, union means a common life; our Lady's life consists chiefly in imparting grace. Her whole life and destiny are behind her motherhood, first of our Lord, and then of mankind. . . . This motherhood of souls being her essential function and her life, it follows that unless we share in it we cannot achieve a real union with her. Real devotion must necessarily include the serving of souls. Mary without her motherhood: a Christian without the apostolic spirit: the two resemble each other. Both alike are incomplete, lacking reality or substance, and would be a distortion of the divine plan. (*Manual of the Legion of Mary,* nos. 191–2.)

Moreover, who can fail to see that this connection between Mary and Catholic Action is a benefit both for the spiritual life and for apostolic activity? It is true that unless a soul is on its guard there is a risk of piety towards our Lady becoming distorted and something too individual, like a closed chapel, something poetical far removed from the prose of daily life: in short into a counterfeit of realistic and virile spirituality. On the other hand, the call to action may arouse only the purely natural instinct of generosity and deviate towards the naturalism which confuses action with agitation and disdains Christian humility. Now who can fail to see the necessity of humility when there is a question of supernatural action? The more humble—deeply humble—a soul, the more does divine grace take possession of it; and the more also is human activity expended in the measure of our fundamental detachment, which maintains and increases humility: the humility of self-sacrifice and of prayer. When devotion to our Lady finds its outlet in apostolic activity, and the activity is rooted in that devotion, what natural and supernatural balance, what fullness is to be seen in this synthesis! And what an understanding also of the vital problems of our time!

As we have said, Mary continues to give to the mystical Body the care she gave to her Son, and such care includes the whole Catholic apostolate whether direct or indirect, whether concerned with undertakings that are definitely religious, with social movements, charitable enterprises, etc. Such is the normal condition of her action. If she finds in us her instruments, then her motherhood can be extended not only to the growth of the divine life in souls, but to all the circumstances which in part condition that growth, as also with all men's bodily sufferings, and all their needs. Then through us she is present in the efforts to spread Christian and Catholic truth by means of the spoken word, by the pen, the radio, television and the cinema. More effective than are we, she is present at all the battles we fight for the cause of God; just as a mother who passionately seeks her children's welfare, and is more concerned with it than they are themselves. She sustains their courage, makes good their deficiencies, and seeks to make the light and warmth of Christ penetrate everywhere, so impatient is her love to open to him the way as soon as she finds the instruments.

Nothing human is alien to her. Queen of peace, be it in

the family, the nation or the world at large, she takes an earnest interest in our private as in our social disputes, and our racial antagonisms. She suffers at the sight of our fratricidal wars. She is present in our missionary undertakings, as Mediatrix of all graces, arousing vocations, obtaining conversions, hastening the day when the Gospel message will be accepted by all to the ends of the earth.

She is present at the centre of the ecumenical movement, she has her part in every effort we expend in order to bring about the union of men of good will by their entry into the Church, which so longs that they may share her unity. Who more than a mother desires and labours to reconcile her strayed children, and to cause them to return to the family home!

Above all, is she present wherever our Lord is still suffering persecution from his enemies, and treading the sorrowful way of the cross, wherever the "Church of Silence" continues to share the agony and passion of her Lord. She is and will be present thus at the centre of the human history of her children, and it is because she wills to be thus everywhere, and share in our entire life, that her spiritual motherhood is ever in action.

THE NECESSARY INITIATION

We have just explained how truly Mary is to be found at the centre of apostolic action and life, but this vision cannot remain an intellectual affair but must pass into practice, be integrated in our teaching and our catechizing. The hiatus between piety and life is still too apparent and must be filled up, and this can be done only by a renewal of the teaching on this vital matter. We can thank God that considerable progress has been made of recent years, both in the psychological adaptation as in the presenting of the value of the content of the teaching, but there is room for

further improvement along the line of the instruction upon
Mary which takes greater account of her universal and
vital part in Christian life.

If we may judge from the majority of the catechisms in
use in different countries, neither Mary nor the apostolic
duty inherent in our baptism has as yet been sufficiently
emphasized. If on the feast of her Nativity, or at a con-
fraternity meeting, there is mention of such, generally
speaking insufficient stress is laid on her part in the other
mysteries, as also on her function as Mediatrix of all
graces. When giving instruction, it is not enough to state a
truth in a general fashion once for all; if we want an idea
really to penetrate into a class, we must keep returning to
it frequently, and seeing it from different angles. Mary is
too much absent from our lessons in doctrine, and overall
views are too much relegated to a particular section, so
that her part seems obscured and accidental. A child must
feel its mother's presence in the home, in every room in
the house, thanks to those many delicate details which
create an atmosphere. Anyone who has been in a home
without a mother understands the distress of orphaned
children. It is enough to put one's finger on this tragic absence of a mother in the Protestant churches to understand
by counterproof the warmth of all-enveloping love which
emanates from her in the Catholic Church. And priests
and leaders of Catholic Action must inculcate that presence in the adults entrusted to them, since grown men and
women must not be left to think that devotion to our Lady
belongs to childish sentimentality and is unsuitable to
those of riper years.

Catholics who have the responsibility of teaching must
aim at making this rôle of Mary thoroughly understood
and appreciated if they want to obtain a really adequate
devotion to our Lady among their pupils. They must likewise emphasize, and sometimes even introduce, a sense of

the apostolic duty binding upon us as baptized Christians. It is not enough to say that we were created to know, love and serve God so long as we do not complete this statement by adding, "and to make him known, loved and served." Otherwise, our Catholic religion will in practice tend to individualism, and apostolic zeal will be regarded as a sort of luxury. We must learn, from our earliest catechism lessons, theoretically and practically, that the Christian is, in Lacordaire's fine definition, "a man to whom God has entrusted other men."

Once Mary's office has been fully recognized, and the imperative duty of leading an apostolic life vigorously inculcated, there will no longer be any difficulty in connecting the two, and of making pass into daily life that duty of corresponding sincerely to that maternity of grace, of which she desires to prolong for our sakes both the efficacy and the benefits. A re-adjustment of life is called for which will be wholly advantageous for the development of the Christian life as God wills it to be lived.

MARY AND THE RENEWAL OF FAMILY LIFE

Not only is our period characterized by a renewal of the sense of apostleship and by a fuller understanding of all that our Lady means to us, but by a better grasp of the spiritual implications of marriage. Mary has her very natural place in this more perfect estimate of love between Christian man and woman which is the instrument of the sanctification of the married couple. As Fr de Lestapis, S.J., very truly wrote: "The mystery of marriage and the family has probably much to learn from the example of Mary and Joseph." We must enter that home at Nazareth in order to find out its message for us today.

At its centre is a woman, Mary, and Joseph her husband, whose union is the most perfect success of earthly love. It is good to search into its secret, for human love will there find its patent of nobility. Excepting only that which existed between Jesus and his Mother, no earthly union was so strong and sacred. The bond between Mary and Joseph was a true marriage and, apart from the procreative act, they belonged wholly to each other and gave themselves wholly to God. "The souls of that man and woman," as Fr Nicolas, O.P., writes, "are associated in order that the image of God may be perfectly reproduced in them. It is good that so great a love, and a love as human as it is divine, should arise and expand in those virgin hearts; for that shows us that purity can leave to the heart its faculty of loving, and that of being united, and that the affection between man and woman can be completely freed from what normally calls it forth and maintains it."

These lines are full of valuable instruction. The truth is that Mary and Joseph raise conjugal life to its highest power, and we must dare to recognize this quite frankly out of respect for the work of God. A timidity which is quite alien from faith has inspired those pious pictures that represent, quite without any evidence, Joseph as an insignificant old man, almost an anonymous personage. This idea rests upon no authority, and on her side Mary is the perfect wife.

Léon Bloy said that the holier a woman is the more womanly she is, and this is especially true in the case of Mary. In her case less than ever does grace destroy nature which, on the other hand, is no obstacle to the love of God which, in this case, entirely dominating the human love, has inspired her resolve to remain a virgin while being at the same time a wife. The moral stature of Joseph was able to share this ideal, and that is enough to prove the affinity existing between their souls, which alike understood the beauty of human love and the incomparable transcendence of God. It is not by abasing the human, by minimizing nature, that they had decided upon this paradoxical synthesis of life, but by carrying the primacy of God to its maximum.

We know that Mary is a mother, but perhaps we have understood less well how truly she is a wife. This side of her life is not a game of make-believe, a convention, but an engagement fully lived out. The Church hails her as "Mother of Fair Love," and that title is verified in every respect. For the glory of Mary, for the realism of our faith, and for the sanctity of marriage, it is necessary to enter into that sanctuary of true love, there to seek inspiration and light.

Mary loved Joseph as no other wife has loved her husband and Joseph was for her unclouded happiness. Their mutual love, lived in full harmony with their vocation, obtained its maximum strength, for the renouncing of all procreation, far from being in their case an obstacle to love, elevated and intensified it, as the banks of a river raise the waters which they canalize and control.

Doubtless, Mary loved all human beings with one and the same supernatural love, which of its nature always gives itself completely. She loved Elizabeth, Zachary and St John, and later on each of the Apostles and each of the holy women. But if the love is the same for all when it is real and founded in God, its intimacy and ways of expressing itself remain variable. Mary gives her heart to each one: tirelessly, without measure, she gives all she can give and at its maximum. But the acceptance of the gift does not depend upon her, and the intensity of the love bestowed will vary according to the capacities of the recipients. Mary could attain to complete intimacy only with Joseph, her husband; Joseph received from her as much as a purely human nature could receive. He knew unequalled intimacy with a love as wide as the world; he was as an aqueduct which receives the whole stream and bears its weight. He was the one person with whom Mary could be herself to the end, with the single reserve of the total continence which, far from being a handicap, purified and enhanced their joy.

Truly does their union remain for all time to come the most delicate living commentary upon the Song of Songs, the purest success of human love and a foretaste of heaven. And yet no intimacy was ever more unselfish than was theirs. With them, we are at the antipodes of all falling back upon self, all exclusiveness. Their mutual love flows forth upon the very immensity of the love of God for the world, since it was directly focused upon Jesus. He was the whole *raison d'être* of their lives. For them literally, to live meant Christ. Their love for him was the centre of all their thoughts, and all their longings, the very breath of their souls. Their entire lives were ordered in view of him; he was the bond of their union, the heart of their hearts, the love that set its seal upon their love. Opening their natures together, in the same rhythm, to the love of the Saviour from whom all began and towards whom all converged, their souls expanded until they were wide as the world.

What a model for any Christian home! Care for others, contact with souls to be saved, is not for baptized souls a sort of spiritual luxury which may be ignored or accepted as we prefer. The very intimacy of conjugal love will be saved and increased only if blown upon by the wind of great apostolic preoccupations. Men who limit their horizon stifle their love instead of cultivating it. Here again, he who loses his life shall save it.

To neglect this worldwide aspect of St Joseph is to do him an injustice. It is there that the cultus paid to him by those devoted to apostolic activity takes its rise, and we must grasp the fact that his worldwide mission is not at an end. The part he played with respect to our Lord he has to continue with respect to the Mystical Body of Christ. Guardian and protector of the former, he must be also of the latter. We do not in practice disassociate the historical and mystical life of our Lord continued in the Church. There is nothing arbitrary in the fact that the popes have proclaimed St Joseph to be the Protector of the Church. His task remains identical through all the changes and chances of this life, and his patronage of Holy Church is but the prolongation of his historical mission. Since the days of Nazareth, the family of God has been enlarged to the dimensions of the world, and St Joseph's heart has been enlarged to the measure of that new fatherhood which prolongs and surpasses that promised by God to Abraham, the father of many nations. God does not act by sudden improvisations, nor by some process of "touching up." Everything is one orderly whole; everything is in a sequence and in continuity. Joseph, the foster-father of Jesus, is such also of the brethren of Jesus who are the Christians through the ages. Husband of Mary, the Mother of Jesus, he remains mysteriously united to her while the mystical birth of the Church pursues its course. There the apostle who is toiling in order to extend here on earth the Kingdom of Heaven, which is the Church, has a right to claim the special protection of that model of the nascent Church which was the Holy Family.

The renewal of conjugal spirituality, which we can see at present, may, therefore, place itself boldly under the sign of that ideal union, and let no one protest that the exclusion of the act of procreation prevents the said union from being at a human level. If the situation of Mary and Joseph was unique in that respect, the fact remains that their union was a success of love. It enables us to understand more clearly how the instinct to reproduce one's kind, and love, those two realities, which are neighbouring but not identical, should be distinguished. Mary and

Joseph offer to the world finished models of love in a state of grace. By their bright example, they reveal to us that Christianity assumes this human value, and is not afraid of love but of its deviations only; since it never forbids men to love too much, but only to love in a manner that is evil.

To further all scientific and pedagogical research which may help man to gain control over and educate his instincts and reflex movements, is to do a work of piety towards our Lady in conformity with her wishes. Such training in true love aims at re-establishing, as far as possible here on earth, the mastery of spirit over body, and that of God over the whole man. And it is all to the benefit of love itself that instead of descending to the level of instinct the latter will rise to the level of love; that is to say, to the level of self-giving and generosity. Mary and Joseph, established by God at a level which is not our own, exercise over us an attraction which uplifts and purifies love in order to detach it from all that is not love, to preserve it from its counterfeits, in order subsequently the better to humanize it.

SELECT BIBLIOGRAPHY

ATTWATER, Donald: *A Dictionary of Mary*, London, Longmans, and New York, Kenedy, 1956.

CONGAR, YVES M.-J., O.P.: *Christ, Our Lady and the Church*, London, Longmans, and Westminster, Md., Newman Press, 1957.

GUITTON, Jean: *The Blessed Virgin*, translated by A. Gordon Smith, London, Burns Oates, 1951, and New York, Kenedy, 1952.

MONTFORT, St Louis Marie Grignon de: *Treatise on the True Devotion to the Blessed Virgin*, Romsey, Montfort College, 1942.

SMITH, George D.: *Mary's Part in Our Redemption*, London, Burns Oates, and New York, Kenedy, 1954.

SUENENS, Léon-Joseph: *Theology of the Apostolate*, Cork, Mercier Press, 1953, and Chicago, Regnery, 1955.

VONIER, Dom Anscar: *The Divine Motherhood*, in Volume I of *The Collected Works,* London, Burns Oates, and Westminster, Md., Newman Press, 1952.

All the papal documents quoted in this volume may be found in: *The Papal Encyclicals in Their Historical Context,* edited by Anne Fremantle, New York, New American Library of World Literature, 1956. See also: *Selected Papal Encyclicals and Letters,* London, Catholic Truth Society, 1939 ——.